# The 4 String Bass to Understanding Music

## A Guide to Understanding Scales, Chords, Arpeggios, and more.

*Written and illustrated by Kevin Delaney*

Copyright © 2010

"Anybody can make the simple complicated.  Creativity is making the complicated simple."

Charles Mingus - Jazz Bassist

# Introduction

If you play the 4 string bass, **The 4 String Bassist's Guide to Understanding Music** will help you to take your bass playing to the next level. This book introduces the bassist to the system of Diatonic Harmony and the scales, modes, chords, and arpeggio patterns that are found throughout the diatonic harmony system. The book uses diagrams and illustrations of the bass fingerboard and the piano keyboard to simplify concepts and identify patterns found in music, and relate these to the 4 string bass. While there is no requirement for the reader to play piano, access to a piano or electronic piano keyboard is beneficial, since the piano is used in addition to the bass fingerboard to provide the reader with a solid understanding of how scales, modes, chords, and arpeggios fit together musically and relate to each other. Also, the book does not require the reader to have the ability to read music. The only requirement is an open mind and the ability to apply the concepts taught here to your own bass playing.

**The 4 String Bassist's Guide to Understanding Music** also introduces Super Scales – the last and only bass fingerboard maps you'll ever need! The Super Scales (presented in both Diatonic and Pentatonic form) greatly simplify the task of memorizing scales and modes in any key. Super Scales cover all four strings of the bass and all octaves, and they are very useful for bassists who improvise when playing.

Many of the concepts discussed throughout the book are commonly taught in college level music theory courses, however, the goal of this book is to simplify these concepts to make them accessible to any bassist who is willing to take the time to read, understand, practice, and apply the material that is presented. While the book is written specifically for bassists who play the 4 string electric bass (fretted or fretless), bassists who play the double (upright acoustic) bass will also benefit from the book.

Thank you and I wish you the best of luck!

Sincerely,

*Kevin Delaney*

# Table of Contents

## Chapter 1: The Basics of the Bass - *page* 1

Tuning your bass ....................................................................................................1
The heart of the bass: The Fingerboard ...................................................................2
Know Your Notes! ...................................................................................................3
Beyond the 12th Fret ...............................................................................................5
The In-Between Notes: Sharps and Flats ..................................................................6
Enharmonic Equivalents ..........................................................................................7
The Parts of the Bass ..............................................................................................8
Treble Clef ............................................................................................................9
Bass Clef ............................................................................................................10
Ledger Lines .......................................................................................................10
The "Ottava" symbol ...........................................................................................11
Location of all notes on the Piano Keyboard ..........................................................11
Location of all notes on the Bass Fingerboard .......................................................13

## Chapter 2: Whole steps and half steps: - *page* 15

Whole Steps and Half Steps at work ......................................................................15
Notes vs. Tones ...................................................................................................15
Finding Middle C ..................................................................................................16
The C Major Scale ...............................................................................................17
Whole Step/Half Step Patterns in the Major Scale ..................................................18
Whole Steps and Half Steps on the Bass ...............................................................19

## Chapter 3: Key Signatures and Scale Construction - *page* 23

The Order of Sharps and the Order of Flats ...........................................................25
Deciphering the Key Signature .............................................................................26
List of Key Signatures ..........................................................................................28

## Chapter 4: Modes - *page* 31

Modes on the Bass Fingerboard ............................................................................34
The "Super Scale" ...............................................................................................35
Analyzing the Super Scale ....................................................................................36
Positions of all modes within the Super Scale ........................................................40
Super Scale in C Major Key Center .......................................................................42
Super Scale in other Key Centers .........................................................................43

## Chapter 5: Seconds & Thirds as Intervals - *page* 45

Major and Minor Thirds on the Bass Fingerboard ...................................................49
Major and Minor Quality .......................................................................................52

## Chapter 6: Triads - *page* 55

    About Triads ..................................................................................................55
    Constructing Triads .........................................................................................55
    Triads as Arpeggios on the Bass Fingerboard ....................................................58
    Combining Major and Minor Thirds as Triads on the Fingerboard .........................59

## Chapter 7: Diatonic Harmony - *page* 65

    Relative Minor .................................................................................................69
    Roman Numerals in Musical Analysis ................................................................72

## Chapter 8: Seventh Chords - *page* 75

    About Seventh Chords .....................................................................................75
    Constructing Seventh Chords ............................................................................75
    The Diatonic Pattern of Seventh Chords ............................................................78
    Chords and Harmony .......................................................................................82

## Chapter 9: Upper Extensions - *page* 85

    Chord Voicings ................................................................................................87

## Chapter 10: Bass Arpeggios using Upper Extensions - *page* 89

    The 1-2-1-2 Arpeggios .....................................................................................91
    The 2-1-2-1 Arpeggios .....................................................................................99

## Chapter 11: The Other Intervals - *page* 109

    Beyond the Octave .........................................................................................111
    More information on Ninths and Tenths ............................................................113

## Chapter 12: Mode and Chord Relationships - *page* 115

    Progressions and Key Centers .........................................................................116

## Chapter 13: The Pentatonic Scale - *page* 119

    The Pentatonic "Super Scale" Pattern ...............................................................122
    Analyzing the Pentatonic Super Scale ..............................................................124

## Chapter 14: Non-Diatonic Notes & Scales - *page* 133

    Blues Notes ...................................................................................................133
    Passing Tones /Passing Notes .........................................................................133
    The Whole Tone Scale ....................................................................................134
    The Chromatic Scale ......................................................................................134
    The Harmonic Minor Scale ..............................................................................135
    The Melodic Minor Scale .................................................................................135

## Conclusion: *page* 137

Chapter 1 - The Basics of the Bass

# Chapter 1: The Basics of the Bass

**Tuning your bass.**

Tuning is critical for musicians. Even the best symphony in the world would sound terrible if all the instruments were out of tune. So when you play your bass with other musicians, you'll want to be in tune with them. While you're learning the bass, the easiest way to keep your bass in tune is an electronic tuner. You can buy an electronic tuner at a local music store. If you're a beginner, using an electronic tuner to tune your bass will also help you to hear the sounds of the bass when the strings are correctly tuned.

The picture below shows the standard tuning of a 4-string bass. The thickest string on the bass is tuned to "E", while the thinnest string is tuned to "G".

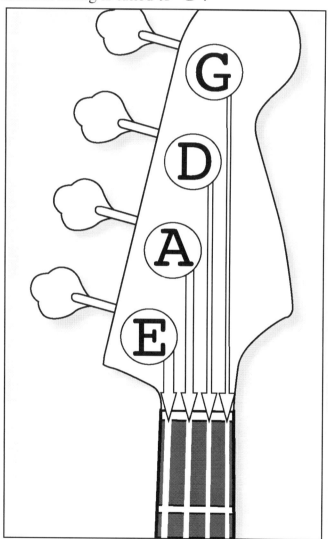

There are several other ways to tune a bass. You can tune using harmonics or by tuning to a guitar or keyboard. Whatever method you choose to tune your bass, keep it in tune.

# The heart of the bass: The Fingerboard.

In the same way a chess player must know the chess board and its pieces, the bassist must know the fingerboard and its scales and notes. Like a chess board, the bass fingerboard also has markings, but on the bass, these markings help you know where the notes reside and where you are when you're playing. The first thing every bassist should know is the location of all the notes on the fingerboard. Before you learn the note names, you'll need to learn the fret numbers. As you'll notice from the picture of the bass fingerboard below, there is a series of dots (some basses have other markers such as squares) - called *fret markers* - on the fingerboard. Below is a diagram showing the fret numbers of the frets that are marked with fret markers.

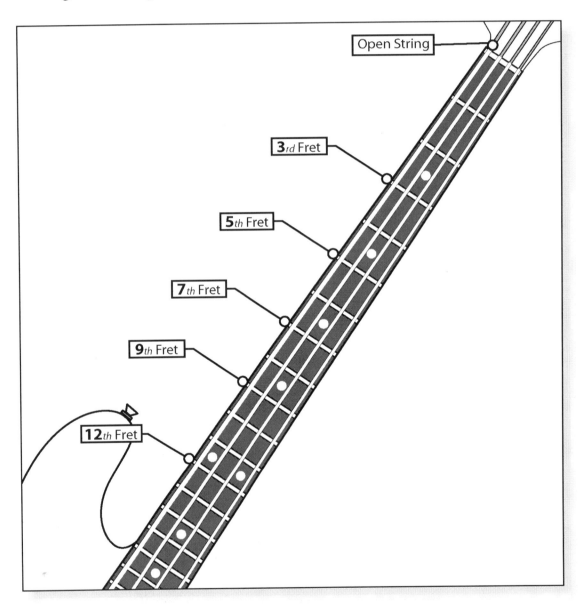

# Know Your Notes!

Knowing the notes of the fingerboard is essential for a bassist to communicate with other musicians. Knowledge of the fingerboard note locations is required when learning to read music, and it will help you to gain a deeper understanding of the world of music. Here's a little story that will help you to remember the locations of the notes on the bass fingerboard. It's a story about a friendly grandmother, who didn't mind having lots of guests over for dinner. When her children and grandchildren came over for dinner, they often asked grandma if they could bring friends along. Grandma never turned anyone away. Here's how Grandma usually responded when she was asked about hosting the extra guests:

Everyone's a dinner guest!
Friends?
Bring 'em all!
Grandma's cookin', folks!
Biscuits...
And darn good chili!
Bring 'em all drinks!
Comfort food!
Bellies expanding!
Darn good chicken fingers!
Everyone's a dinner guest!

SUPER cheesy, without a doubt, but as you can see from the notes positioned on the fingerboard, each line of the story represents the corresponding note groups on the fingerboard.

Notice where these notes fall in relation to the fret numbers.

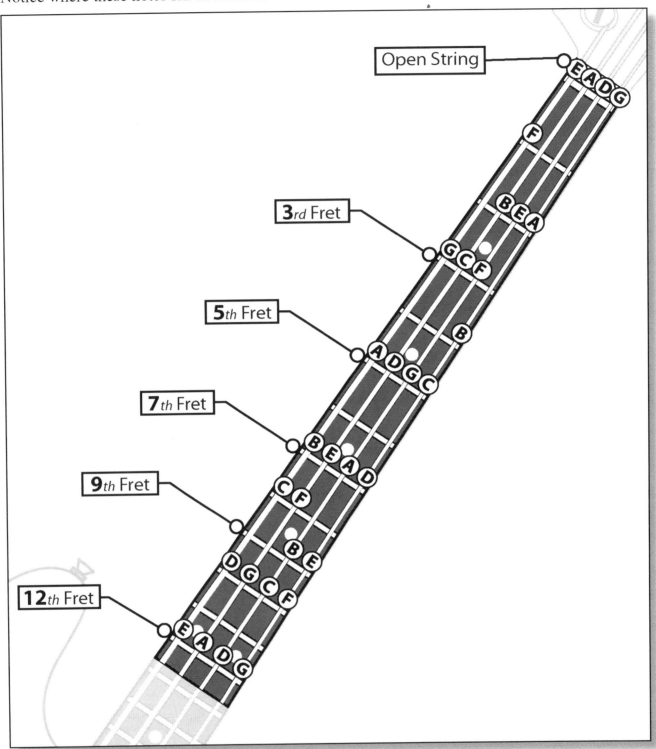

While the diagram above stops at the 12th fret, it's important to be aware the notes repeat from the 12th fret through the remaining frets, and different basses have different numbers of frets. Some basses have 20 frets, some have 21 frets, some have 24 frets.

Chapter 1 - The Basics of the Bass - Know Your Notes

# Beyond the 12th Fret

Below is a diagram showing the positions of the bass notes on the frets starting at the 12th fret and beyond. If you plan to play a lot of the notes beyond the 12th fret, you should definitely know the names of all the notes beyond the 12th fret on your bass.

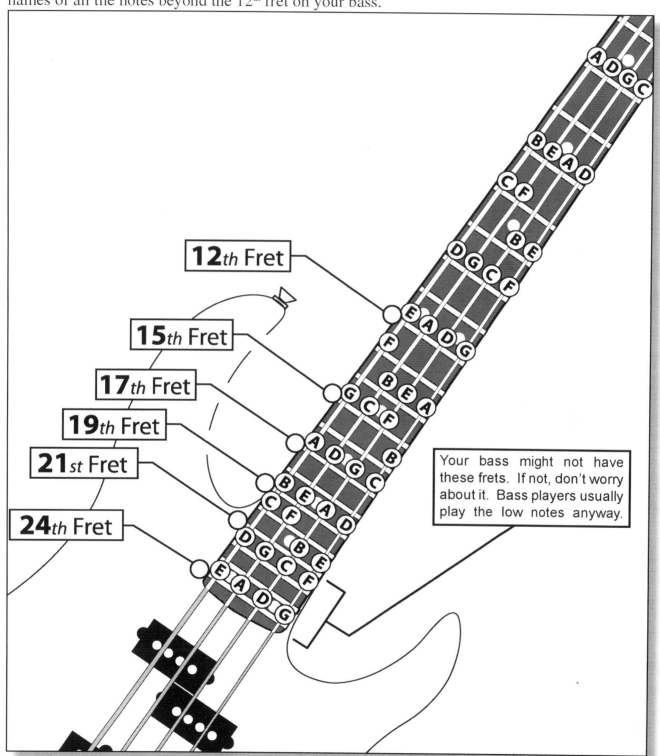

Your bass might not have these frets. If not, don't worry about it. Bass players usually play the low notes anyway.

Chapter 1 - The Basics of the Bass - Beyond the 12th Fret

# The In-Between Notes: Sharps and Flats

All notes in the previous examples are called "natural" notes. The terms "Sharp" or "Flat" describe a change to the pitch of a natural note. The term "Sharp" describes the *raising* of the pitch of a natural note to the next possible note *above*, while the term "Flat" describes the *lowering* of the pitch of a natural note to the next possible note *below*. Here's an example using the D note:

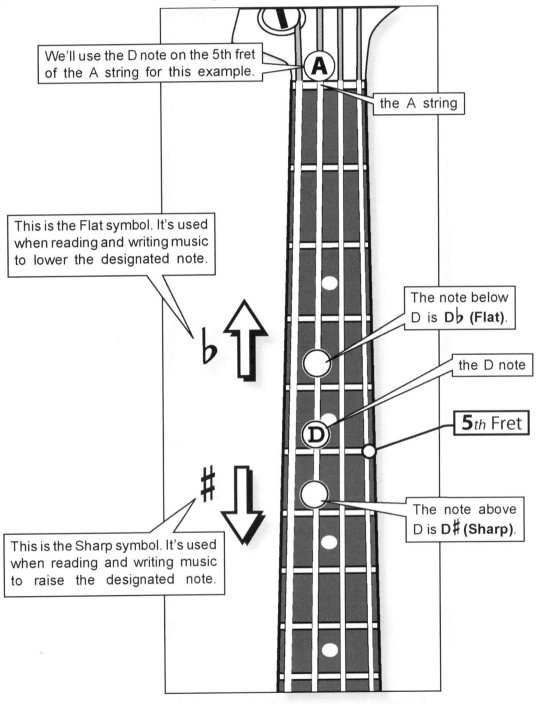

# Enharmonic Equivalents

The term "Enharmonic Equivalent" is a term that refers to different note *names* which, when played, are actually the same note (or pitch). This is something that is known by music nerds everywhere, so if you admit to knowing about enharmonic equivalents, you'll be exposed as a music nerd. Nerdy or not, you should be aware of this. Below is an example:

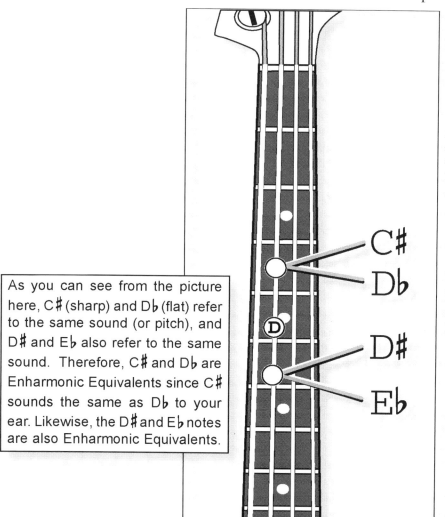

As you can see from the picture here, C♯ (sharp) and D♭ (flat) refer to the same sound (or pitch), and D♯ and E♭ also refer to the same sound. Therefore, C♯ and D♭ are Enharmonic Equivalents since C♯ sounds the same as D♭ to your ear. Likewise, the D♯ and E♭ notes are also Enharmonic Equivalents.

When using sharps and flats, some notes become confusing when altered with a sharp or a flat. These are the notes where there's a natural note directly above or below. (This distance to the note directly above or below a note is referred to as a distance of a Half Step - more on half steps later). For example, the note C is directly above the B note, so modifying the B note with a sharp (♯) changes the pitch to B♯ which is the "enharmonic equivalent" of C. The same holds true for E♯ which is the enharmonic equivalent of F. On the other hand, C♭ (flat) is the enharmonic equivalent of B and F♭ is the enharmonic equivalent of E. As you can imagine, this can be very confusing to a musician who is reading a musical composition, so composers sometimes avoid writing music in keys which include B♯, C♭, E♯, or F♭.

# The Parts of the Bass

Before we move on to the basics of music, take a look at the picture below showing the names of the various parts of the bass.

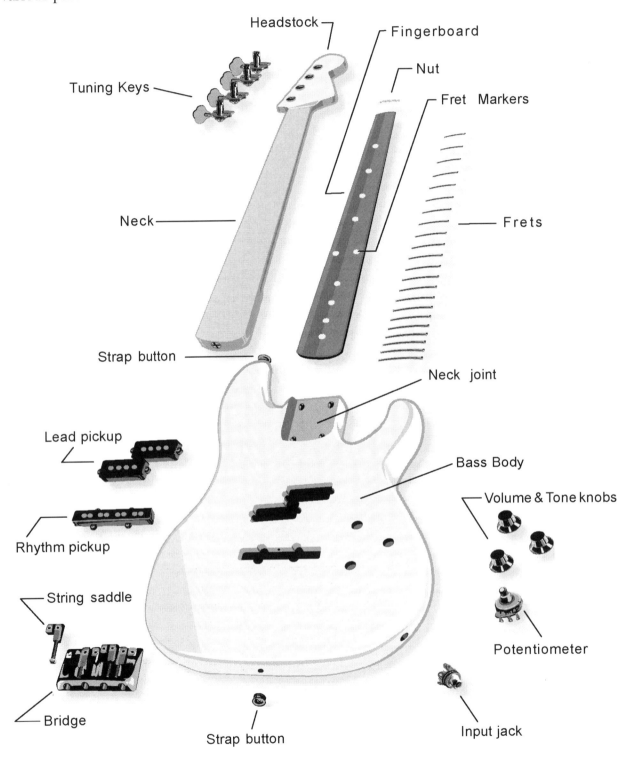

# Treble and Bass Clef

Bassists normally use only the Bass Clef when reading music. However, if you're serious about reading music, you should also be familiar with the Treble Clef. This section will cover the note positions on the bass and treble clefs.

# Treble Clef

If you have ever studied piano, you probably know the notes on the treble clef very well. While bassists normally use the bass clef when reading music, the treble clef is utilized by many instruments, so it's a good idea to be familiar with it. Musicians like to make up phrases that help them remember the note names in various musical situations, and the treble and bass clefs are no exception. Take a look at the illustrations below and memorize the note positions using the two phrases provided:

## Treble Clef Lines

From the bottom **line** and going up, the lines of the treble clef represent the notes:

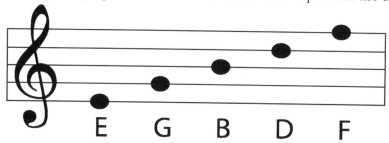

The phrase commonly used to recall the notes associated with the *lines* of the treble clef, from the bottom line going up is:

"**E**very **G**ood **B**oy **D**eserves **F**udge".

## Treble Clef Spaces

From the bottom **space** and going up, the spaces of the treble clef notes represent:

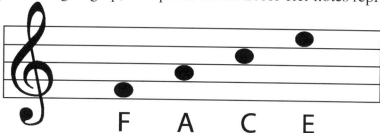

From the bottom space and going up, the phrase commonly used to recall the notes associated with the spaces of the treble clef is simply the word "**face**".

Important: Notice that these note names go from the bottom of the staff to the top of the staff.

## Bass Clef

From the bottom **line** and going up, the lines of the bass clef represent the notes:

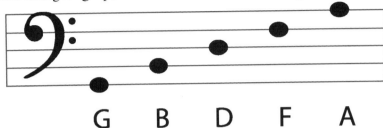

The phrase commonly used to recall the notes associated with the lines of the bass clef is: "**G**ood **B**oys **D**o **F**ine **A**lways" – or, if you prefer, "**G**old **B**ars **D**on't **F**ly **A**way".

From the bottom **space** and going up, the spaces of the bass clef spell out the notes:

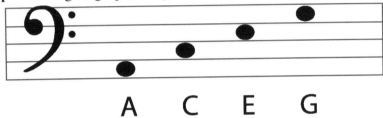

The phrase commonly used to recall the notes associated with the spaces of the bass clef is: "**A**ll **C**ows **E**at **G**rass".

Again, notice that these note names go from the bottom of the staff to the top of the staff.

## Ledger Lines

As you can imagine, there are more notes on the piano or the bass than the 9 that are covered by the spaces and lines of either treble or bass clef. In order to accommodate for these additional notes, musicians use Ledger Lines. These ledger lines represent notes that are higher or lower than those contained in the staff.

The illustrations below show the definitions of the ledger lines and spaces above and below the treble clef.

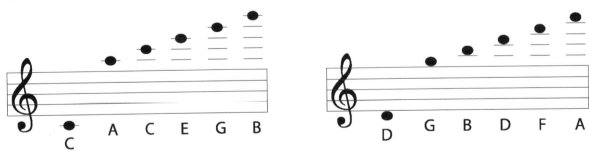

The ledger line just below the treble clef represents Middle C on the piano; you'll learn about Middle C in the next chapter.

The illustrations below show the definitions of the ledger lines above and below the bass clef.

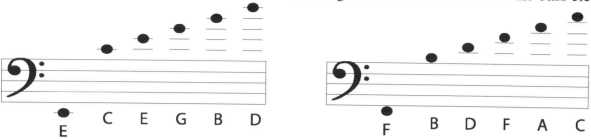

Notes for bass are written an octave above their actual tone (when matched with the keyboard.) This is called "transposing". Transposition is used to allow most of the notes that the musician reads to fall on the staff rather than the ledger lines. Imagine trying to read the following phrase:

While this phrase is written for bass in the actual position of the same tones on the piano, it is very difficult to read because of the ledger lines.

Now look at the same phrase transposed (moved and re-written) up one octave:

Much easier to read because most of the notes fall on the bass clef staff. This is the reason we transpose when writing music for the bass. (If you can't read these examples of musical notation, don't worry, you can still learn from this book; it's oriented toward non-music readers who seek a better understanding of music.)

## The "Ottava" symbol

Another method used to contain notes within the staff (rather than on ledger lines) in written music is the "Ottava" (or 8va.) symbol. The Ottava symbol (*the word "ottava" means "octave" in Italian, which is the language used for most musical terms*) looks like this:

In this example, the 8va. sign above the staff tells the reading musician to play the notes indicated by the line to the right of the 8va. symbol an octave *above* the written notes. (An 8va. symbol below the notes would tell the reading musician to play the notes an octave *lower* than written.)

Now that you know the notes of the treble and bass clefs, let's take a close look at the position of the notes on the piano keyboard.

# Location of all notes on the Piano Keyboard

The piano keyboard is often the starting point for teaching music theory and harmony. In order to gain a better understanding of music, you should therefore know the notes on the piano keyboard. Study the diagram below, and more importantly, play each note on the piano and listen to how each note sounds in relation to the notes around it. (Remember, the ♯ symbol means "sharp" and the ♭ symbol means "flat".)

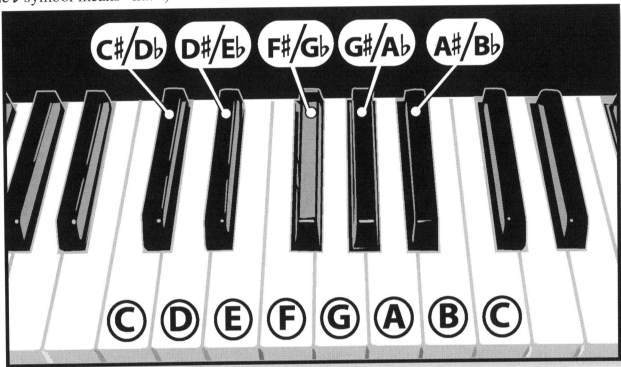

Notice that E♯, F♭, B♯, and C♭ are not shown here. This is because E♯ is equivalent to F, F♭ is equivalent to E, B♯ is equivalent to C, and C♭ is equivalent to B. Not to say there is no such thing as E♯, F♭, B♯, and C♭. But they can lead to confusion, so most composers tend to avoid key signatures that include E♯, F♭, B♯, and C♭. So just be aware that E♯, F♭, B♯, and C♭ do exist. Also, be aware that the notes shown above repeat on the piano in different octaves. (See below)

The asterisks (*) denote the repetition of the C note in octaves on the piano keyboard. Be aware that the note named "C" can appear numerous times on a piano. However, the pitch of these numerous "C" notes can range from low to high.

# Location of all notes on the Bass Fingerboard

Knowing how to locate the positions of the Sharp and Flat notes on the bass fingerboard will be important to a complete understanding of Key Signatures as they relate to the bass. If you know the positions of the Natural notes on the bass fingerboard, you can easily locate the Sharp and Flat notes, since a Sharp note is the next fret up from the related natural note and a Flat note is the next fret down from the related natural note. Keep in mind the word "Natural" refers to a note in its natural state, unaltered by a Sharp or Flat symbol. There is also a symbol for designating natural notes in written music.

That symbol (also called a "natural sign") looks like this: ♮

The note between F and G can be called either F♯ or G♭

The note between G and A can be called either G♯ or A♭

The note between A and B can be called either A♯ or B♭

The note between C and D can be called either C♯ or D♭

The note between D and E can be called either D♯ or E♭

While the example here shows the position of the Sharp and Flat notes in the first octave of the "E" string, the same rule holds true for the rest of the fingerboard: Sharp notes are the next fret up from the natural notes and the Flat notes are the next fret down from the natural notes.

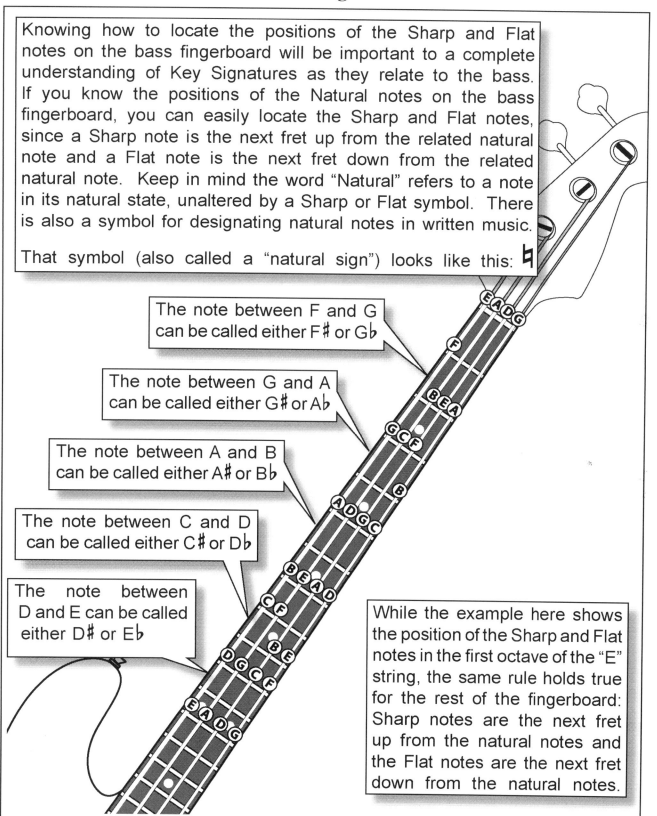

Chapter 1 - The Basics of the Bass - Location of all notes on the Bass Fingerboard

Chapter 2 - Whole Steps and Half Steps

# Chapter 2: Whole steps and half steps: The basic building blocks of scales & chords

The basic building blocks for Western music are the half step and the whole step. The term "Western Music," as used here, refers to the music of Western societies, as opposed to the music of Eastern societies, where the quarter tone is the basic building block of music. Whole steps and half steps represent the basic units used to measure the distance from one note to another. Scales are built using combinations of whole steps and half steps. Chords are constructed using intervals called "Thirds," which are also built up from whole steps and half steps.

## Whole Steps and Half Steps at work

If you have access to a piano, you can see, and more importantly hear, whole steps and half steps at work. Most people in Western society are familiar with the sound of the "solfa" syllables – Do, Re, Mi, Fa, Sol, La, Ti, Do. What you should understand as a musician is that the "Do-Re-Mi..." sound is based on a major scale, and that scale is a sequence of whole steps and half steps. We'll be looking at the C Major Scale as a starting point for analyzing whole steps and half steps as they fit in the Major Scale. We'll use the C Major Scale because it contains only the "Natural" notes. On the piano, these natural notes are the white keys on the keyboard. And in order to get the Do-Re-Mi sound – or the sound of a Major scale, while playing only the white keys on the piano, you must start at the note named "C", and move in order from left to right, creating the sound of the C major scale.

So, in order to analyze the C major scale, we'll turn first to the piano keyboard because it will allow us to clearly see the whole step/half step patterns in the scale. The benefit of the piano for musical analysis requires a bit of explanation, so before we take a closer look at the C Major scale, here's a very brief explanation of why a bass book relies so heavily on piano:

First, the piano is considered the "Hub" of Western Harmony. This is because the piano provides the player with the ability to create Melody and Harmony at the same time. Melody can be defined as a series of notes played one note at a time. Harmony is many notes sounding simultaneously; impossible for many instruments such as violin, saxophone, or trumpet, to accomplish while played solo. Composers have exploited the capability of the keyboard to play melody and harmony for centuries. (The only other instrument that even comes close is the guitar.) Just consider the great composers - Bach, Mozart, Beethoven - all of them experts at the keyboard. Additionally, the keyboard is laid out very logically. This layout makes it much easier to explain some of the concepts that will ultimately deepen your understanding of the bass, and that's why this lesson (and the book) incorporates the keyboard.

## Notes vs. Tones

For the duration of this lesson, we'll be referring to both Notes and Tones: The word "note" refers to the alphabet letter name that you assign to a given tone - alphabetical names ranging from A to G are assigned to the various tones. The word "tone" refers to the sound you hear when you press a key on the piano, blow a trumpet, or pluck a string on a bass.

# Finding Middle C

Western Harmony is based on a 12 tone system. For further explanation, we'll look at the 12 tones between Middle C and the C one octave above Middle C. ("Middle C" is the C in the middle of the keyboard.) To hear a C Major scale in action, locate "Middle C", which is normally found at the center of the keyboard and it is most often located below the first letter of the piano manufacturers name. (*See example below*)

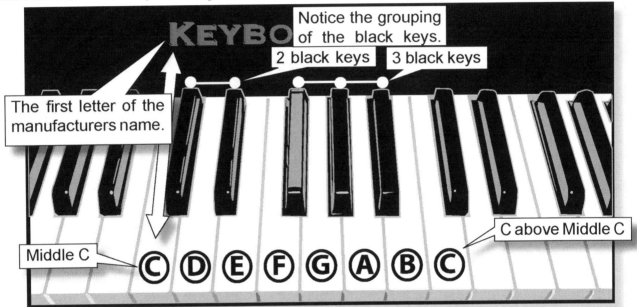

Once you've located it, press the middle C key and then press the white key to the right of the previous key until you reach the C above middle C. You should hear the "Do-Re-Mi" scale. There are 7 note names on the white keys at the Middle C octave. They are C, D, E, F, G, A, B. Regarding the black keys, these represent the 5 remaining tones in the 12 tone system that fall between the notes listed above. The function of these black keys will be covered in detail in later lessons. Notice that the note name of the number 8 tone (also called the "octave") is the same note name as the number 1 tone (sometimes called the "tonic" note).

Now here's something you should be aware of – some white keys don't have black keys between them – this occurs where there are naturally occurring half steps, and that's one feature of the piano keyboard that makes it the ideal instrument for explaining the very basics of music theory. Understanding the placement of half steps and whole steps is a good starting point for anyone wishing to expand their understanding of music.

In addition to understanding and recognizing the Do-Re-Mi sound of the C Major Scale, you will also need to be aware of the usefulness of applying numbers to the steps of the scale for the purpose of analysis. These numbers are useful because patterns that emerge when using these numbers can be applied regardless of the key center. This will require more explanation, but you should definitely be aware that music theory also relies on a numbering system to identify specific patterns that occur. The following illustration shows both the notes of the C Major Scale and the numbering system used in music theory in its most basic form.

# The C Major Scale

The picture below shows the note names (and scale step numbers) and the location of whole steps and half steps within a C Major scale:

The diagram above shows several things:
- *Names of the notes (C, D, E...)*
- *Numbers associated with the scale steps (1, 2, 3...)*
- *The Whole Step/Half Step pattern found in the Major Scale*

Also notice that the grouping of 2 black keys falls between notes C, D, & E while the grouping of 3 black keys falls between notes F, G, A, & B. This pattern repeats on the keyboard throughout all octaves. While the octaves and the tones change, the note names remain the same. This consistent pattern is another reason that the piano keyboard is an excellent tool for use when explaining the patterns found in music. Also, notice that on the keyboard, in the key of C Major, if two white keys have a black key between them, they are a Whole Step apart. If two white keys do not have a black key between them, they are a Half Step apart.

# Whole Step/Half Step Patterns in the Major Scale

The C Major Scale contains a specific pattern that is very important to understanding music theory. Take note of the following:

> **Because there are no black keys between notes E & F or B & C, there are naturally occurring Half Steps between these notes.**

So, there are Half Steps between:
- E & F
- B & C

There are Whole Steps between:
- C & D
- D & E
- F & G
- G & A
- A & B

Regarding the scale step numbers (when applied to a Major Scale):
There are Half Steps between scale steps:
- 3 & 4
- 7 & 8

There are Whole Steps between scale steps:
- 1 & 2
- 2 & 3
- 4 & 5
- 5 & 6
- 6 & 7

Let's look at this another way, with note names and step numbers running parallel:

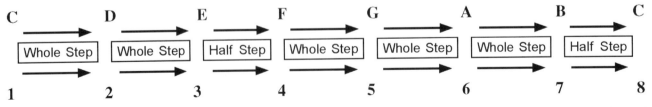

The examples above show that in the C Major scale, there are half steps between notes E & F, and notes B & C. They also show that when using numbers to identify scale steps in a Major scale, there are half steps between step numbers 3 & 4, and step numbers 7 & 8. This pattern - half steps between 3 & 4 and 7 & 8 - is very important and will be used later when creating major scales in other keys. Adhering to this half step/whole step pattern is the reason we use Key Signatures when creating major scales in keys other than C major… more on key signatures later.

# Whole Steps and Half Steps on the Bass

There is more than one way to play a whole step or a half step on the bass fingerboard. Whether you are learning music theory or just learning to play the bass, playing scales is often a starting point. Since scales are built of whole steps and half steps, and understanding diatonic harmony starts with an understanding of whole steps and half steps, it's important to know how to recognize whole steps and half steps on the bass fingerboard. The following examples show two ways to play whole steps and two ways to play half steps on the bass fingerboard. We will use all of these whole steps and half steps whether studying the basics of diatonic harmony or creating scales.

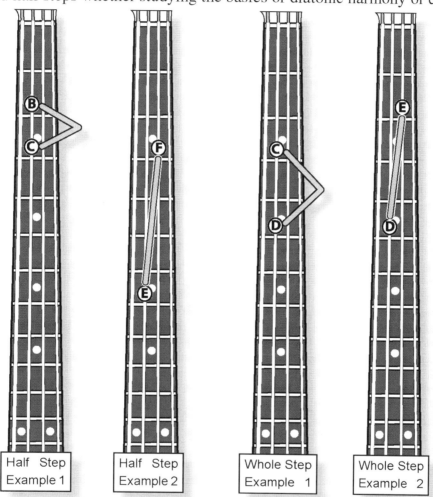

Notice that the half step in *Half Step Example 1* refers to a distance between two separate notes located on the same string. *Half Step Example 2* shows the shape of a Half Step between two strings when you cross from one string to the adjacent string on the bass fingerboard. The whole step shown in *Whole Step Example 1* refers to a distance between two separate notes that are located on the same string – notice these 2 notes are separated by an unused fret on the fingerboard. *Whole Step Example 2* shows the shape of a Whole Step between two strings when you cross from one string to the adjacent string on the bass fingerboard.

Once you understand the whole step and the half step as a building block, you're ready to learn to analyze scales. A normal starting point for most bass students when learning scales is the C Major Scale. This scale is the Do-Re-Mi scale we discussed earlier. Now that we've reviewed the C Major Scale on the keyboard, and we've seen the different ways to play whole steps and half steps on the bass fingerboard, here are several ways to play a C major scale on a bass. (Play these scale examples in order of the note names – C, D, E, F, G, A, B, C):

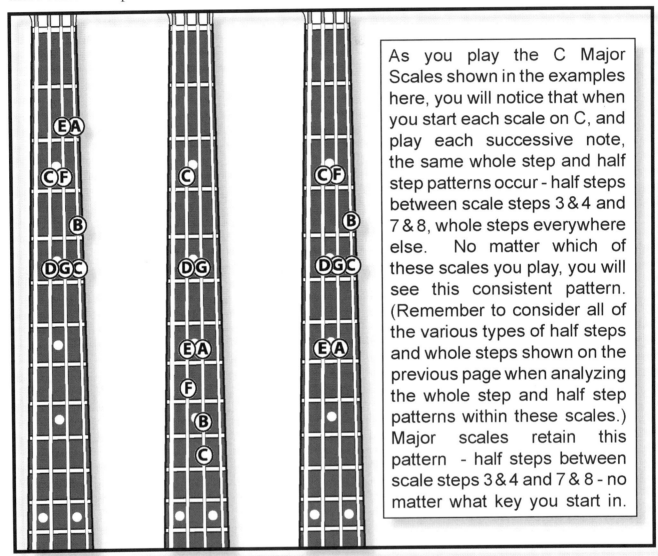

As you play the C Major Scales shown in the examples here, you will notice that when you start each scale on C, and play each successive note, the same whole step and half step patterns occur - half steps between scale steps 3 & 4 and 7 & 8, whole steps everywhere else. No matter which of these scales you play, you will see this consistent pattern. (Remember to consider all of the various types of half steps and whole steps shown on the previous page when analyzing the whole step and half step patterns within these scales.) Major scales retain this pattern - half steps between scale steps 3 & 4 and 7 & 8 - no matter what key you start in.

Of course there are many more ways to play a C Major scale on the bass. However, on the piano, there is only one way. This is the primary reason that a basic understanding of the piano keyboard is important to a simplified understanding of music.

It is important to understand that, as building blocks, 2 half-steps, when combined, equal one whole step. This becomes important when you start building scales in keys other than C Major. For example, if you play the note E, then move to the note, F, you play a half-step. In order to play a whole step above the E note, you need to play the note a half-step above F, or F♯. So, from E to F is a half-step, and F to F♯ is a half-step, but the interval (distance) from E to F♯ is a whole-step.

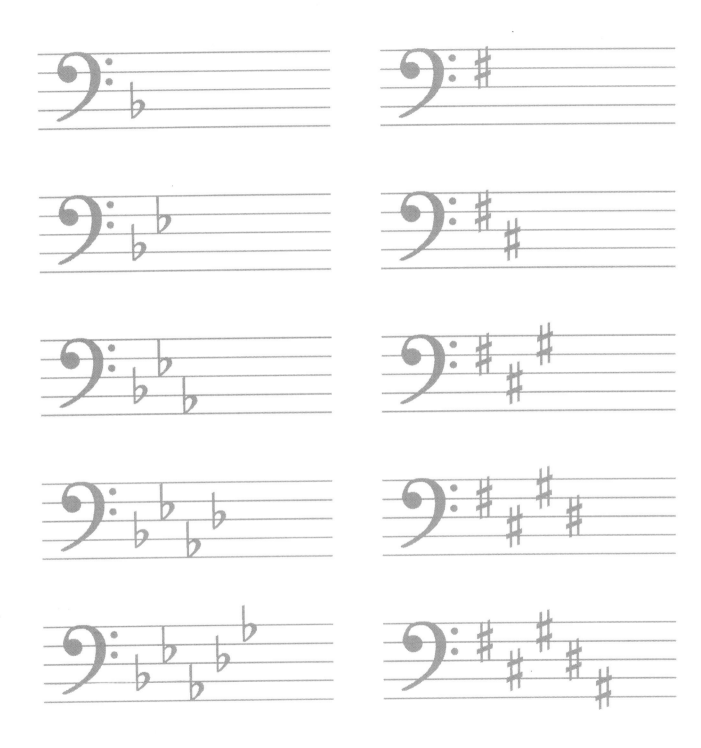

Chapter 3 - Key Signatures

# Chapter 3: Key Signatures and Scale Construction

In Chapter 1, we reviewed sharps and flats on the keyboard and the bass, and in Chapter 2, we learned about the whole step and half step pattern of the Major scale. Now let's take a look at Key Signatures. Remember the "Do-Re-Mi" thing that we call a Major scale? Well, in order to make sure that half steps occur between scale steps 3 & 4 and 7 & 8 when starting a Major scale on notes other than C, we'll need to use *Sharp* or *Flat* notes. On the piano keyboard, which we'll use to illustrate the principles discussed here, when starting a Major scale on notes other than C, some of the notes on the white keys need to be moved up or down a half step in order to maintain the whole step and half step pattern of the Major scale. This brings the black keys on the keyboard - the sharps and flats - into play. A *Sharp* note is the note a half step *above* a given natural note while a *Flat* note is the note a half step *below* a given natural note.

When using sharps and flats to create Major scales, keep in mind these rules:

- The Major Scale maintains half steps between scale step numbers 3 & 4 and 7 & 8, with whole steps between the remaining notes.

- When writing the notes of a scale, each note letter must be represented only once. For example, an A Major scale would include these notes – A, B, C♯, D, E, F♯, G♯, A. So, you would never write: A, B, D♭, D, E, F♯, G♯, A – in this example, the letter D is repeated twice, and the letter C is not present (even though D♭ sounds the same as C♯.)

- Never mix Sharps and Flats as shown in the following incorrect example: A, B♭, C, D, E, F♯, G♯, A - This example incorrectly contains both sharps and flats. *The only exception to this rule would be the Harmonic and Melodic Minor scales, which are modified "hybrid" scales. For basic Diatonic scales, don't mix sharps and flats in the same scale, and never mix them in the key signature.*

**Below are a few examples of key signatures on the bass clef.**

Key Signatures are found at the beginning of a piece of written music, and they tell the musician which notes throughout that music are modified by the sharps or flats found in the key signature. In this book, we'll be using key signatures for the purpose of furthering our knowledge of scale construction and Diatonic Harmony.

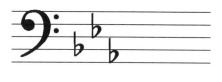

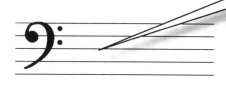

If there are no sharps or flats in a key signature, the music is probably written in C Major - recall that the C Major scale is comprised of all "Natural" notes, and no sharps or flats.

So, let's create a major scale starting on a note other than C. Let's start with G on the piano keyboard. If we construct the scale slowly and observe the requirement to maintain whole steps everywhere except scale steps 3 & 4 and 7 & 8, where half-steps are required (for the construction of a Major scale), we'll find that a sharp is required - F♯ - in order to maintain a half-step between scale steps 7 & 8. This is basically where Key Signatures come from.

G *to* A – 1 *to* 2 – whole step
A *to* B – 2 *to* 3 – whole step
B *to* C – 3 *to* 4 – half step
C *to* D – 4 *to* 5 – whole step
D *to* E – 5 *to* 6 – whole step
E *to* F♯ – 6 *to* 7 – whole step
F♯ *to* G – 7 *to* 8 – half step

So as you can see, building a Major scale starting on notes other than C requires that you modify notes with sharps or flats. In the case of the G Major scale, an F♯ is required.

## The Function of Key Signatures

One of the primary functions of a key signature is to facilitate the construction of Major scales starting on any of the 12 available tones. Key signatures also guide the reading musician to play the correct notes in a written composition. Key signatures can also be analyzed to show patterns that can help you gain a better understanding of the system referred to as Diatonic Harmony. In brief, Diatonic Harmony is the study and analysis of musical scales, starting with the Major Scale, and extending that Major Scale into modes (sub-scales of the Major Scale) and chords (the foundation of harmony) in order to find consistent patterns that occur in music, regardless of the Key Center. A basic understanding of Diatonic Harmony is critical to the serious bassist.

The rules of the Diatonic Harmony system are not infinite. In fact, many of them come in groups of seven. Why seven? Well, there are seven note names in music – A, B, C, D, E, F, and G. There are seven notes in the Major scale. There are basically seven diatonic chords built upon the seven steps of the Major scale. There are seven Sharp key signatures and seven Flat key signatures. There are seven "modes" of the Major scale (including the Major scale itself). Modes are sub-scales of the Major scale. These modal scales are derived using only the seven tones/notes in the related Major scale - each mode starts on one of the seven scale steps, with a new whole step and half step pattern. (Later, we'll learn the ancient Greek names for these modes.)

Fully understanding Diatonic Harmony requires that you know the Major scales in all keys. Knowing the Major scales in all keys requires that you learn all of the key signatures. Remember, there are only seven Sharp key signatures and seven Flat key signatures to learn. Therefore, the next lesson discusses a couple of tricks that will help you learn and remember all of the key signatures.

# The Order of Sharps and the Order of Flats.

Sharps (represented by the ♯ symbol) appear in the Key Signature in the following order:

**F, C, G, D, A, E, B**

Here's a little saying to help you remember the order of sharps:
> ***Father Christmas Gave Dad An Electric Bass***

Flats (represented by the ♭ symbol) appear in the Key Signature in the following order:

**B, E, A, D, G, C, F**

Here's a little saying to help you remember the order of flats:
> ***Bass Exploded And Dad Got Cranky Fast***

Sharps and Flats ALWAYS occur in this order!! Note that **F C G D A E B** is **B E A D G C F** backwards, and vice versa. Also notice that these two sayings combine to tell the following tale:

> **Father Christmas Gave Dad An Electric Bass**
> **Bass Exploded And Dad Got Cranky Fast**

When it comes to key signatures, Sharps and Flats are always written on the staff in a specific order. The sharp and flat symbols are always placed on the staff in the area that's reserved for the key signature. If you've looked at a variety of written music, you've probably seen various key signatures on the pages. It's important to be able to recognize what key center the key signature is referring to. (For now, the term "key center" will refer to a given Major scale and its associated modes and chords.) Rather than memorizing the number of sharps or flats in a key signature to determine the "key center" from memory, musicians sometimes use a trick to help quickly determine the key of a given piece of music, as we'll see on the next page.

> The term Key Center will require more advanced explanation later because it could mean many things, depending on if the music is written in a Major key, a Minor key, or a with modal key center. This is a bare bones crash course on music theory for the bassist. A full explanation of music theory requires a college level course or a private instructor. So, as a starting point, we will be referring to Major keys when learning to identify the key center of a key signature. However, you should be aware that the most widely used alternative to writing music in a Major key is to write music in a "Relative Minor" key, which is a Minor key that's "related" to a Major key – hence the term "relative" Minor. The Relative Minor key is based on the Natural Minor scale – a mode (or sub-scale) built on the 6th step of the Major scale. So as you become more experienced with written music, you will need to be aware that a key signature which appears to identify a Major key could actually be the key center that is based on the Relative Minor of that Major key signature. The Relative Minor Key is based on the Natural Minor Scale, which we will cover later when we learn about modes.

# Deciphering the Key Signature

Knowing the Order of Sharps and Flats can help you determine the Key Center of a piece of music when you see that key signature in written music. By using some simple tricks, you can learn to look at the key signature and determine the key center of that music. As mentioned previously, determining whether a piece has a Major, Relative Minor, or Modal Key Center takes experience. So we'll start by learning the trick used to determine the key center of Major key signatures.

**To determine the Major key center of a Key Signature containing Sharps (♯):**

*When determining the Key Signature from the order of Sharps:*

> ## The last sharp in the key signature is the seventh note of the Major scale

The seventh note of the Major scale, is also referred to as the "leading tone" because sonically, it leads the ear back to the "Root" note, also referred to as the "tonic", or Key Center tone. Conversely, the root note is a half step above the 7th note.

*Here's how you use this knowledge:*

You see a piece of sheet music with 2 sharps – F♯ and C♯. Following the order of sharps, F♯ comes first, and C♯ is next. There are only 2 sharps in the Key Signature, and C♯ is the last sharp in this example, and therefore C♯ is the seventh note of a Major scale. And since there's a half step between scale steps 7 & 8 in a Major scale, C♯ - the seventh note - is a half step below D, which is the "8" note (or octave).

So a piece of music that contains two sharps in the key signature is written in the key of D Major. By playing notes, D, E, F♯, G, A, B, C♯, D, on the piano keyboard, you'll see that when you start a scale on D, and you maintain half steps between scale steps 3 & 4 and 7 & 8, you create a scale where F and C are both sharp (♯).

Similarly, if the key signature shows 3 sharps, following the order of sharps tells you that these sharps are F♯, C♯, and G♯. Since G♯ is the last sharp in this example, and therefore the seventh note in the Major scale, we can determine that the eighth note of the scale is **A**. By playing the notes, A, B, C♯, D, E, F♯, G♯, A, on the piano keyboard, you'll see that when you start a scale on the A note, and you maintain half steps between scale steps 3 & 4 and 7 & 8,

you create a scale where F is sharp, C is sharp, and G is sharp. As you can hear (*if you played the example*) and see (*in the illustration*), an A Major scale does in fact have 3 sharps: F♯, C♯, and G♯.

## To determine the Major key center of a Key Signature which contains Flats (♭):

The rule for flats has one exception – the key of F Major, which has one flat - B flat (B♭). B♭ is the first in the Order of Flats. The trick you're about to learn for determining the Major Key Center of a piece of music with a key signature that contains flats doesn't apply to the key of F Major. You should memorize the fact that one flat - B flat (B♭) in the key signature represents the Key of F Major. As for the other keys, here's how you can determine which Major key is represented when you see flats in the key signature:

*When determining the Key Signature from the order of Flats:*

> ### The second to last flat in the key signature is the key center (or root).

*Here's how you use this knowledge:*

If you see a piece of sheet music with 2 flats in the key signature, by utilizing the order of flats, you'll know those 2 flats are B♭ and E♭. Since the last flat in this key signature is E♭, we know the second to last flat in this example is B♭.

So the Major Key center here is B♭. By playing the notes, B♭, C, D, E♭, F, G, A, B♭, on the piano keyboard and by maintaining half steps between scale steps 3 & 4 and 7 & 8, you'll see that starting a scale on the B♭ note results in a Major scale where B is flat and E is flat.

To take this one step further, let's analyze a key signature with 3 flats. Since the order of flats doesn't change, these 3 flats will be B♭, E♭, and A♭. So A♭ is the last flat in a key signature with 3 flats, E♭ is the second to last flat, and the second to last flat is the Root of the Major scale - E♭ in this case. Therefore, we know that a key signature with 3

flats represents the key of E♭ Major. By constructing a scale on the piano keyboard starting on the E♭ note and adhering to the pattern of maintaining half steps between scale steps 3 & 4 and 7 & 8, we create a scale that contains the following notes: E♭, F, G, A♭, B♭, C, D, E♭. As you can hear *(if you played the example)* and see in the illustration, an E♭ Major scale does in fact have 3 flats: B♭, E♭, and A♭.

# List of Key Signatures

Here is a list of the Key Signatures:

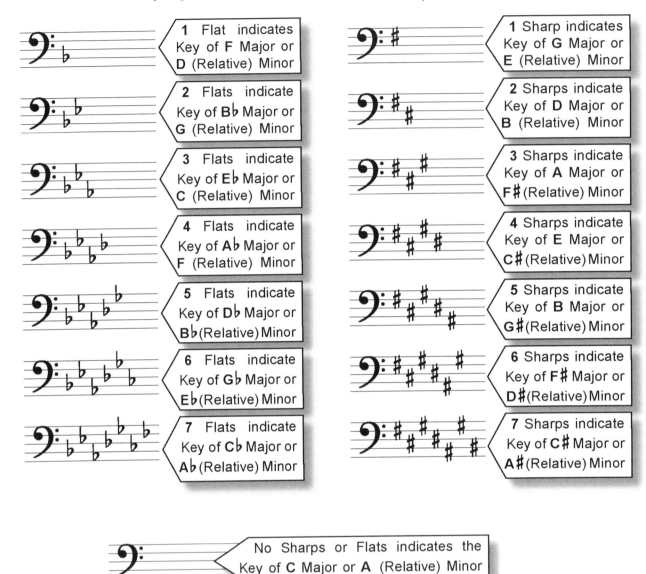

Practice building Major scales in the keys named above using a piano keyboard (if you have access to one). Building Major scales on the piano will challenge you to think in terms of not only the key signature, but the whole step and half step patterns required to construct Major scales in the various keys. Also, build these same scales on the bass, but don't just play patterns - visualize each note name and its position on the fingerboard as you play. Be aware that keys with 6 or 7 Flats can include the notes C♭ or F♭ (or both). If you play C♭ (the note a half-step below C) on the piano, you'll notice that it is actually B you're playing. In the same way, playing an F♭ is equivalent to playing an E. Additionally, keys with 6 or 7 Sharps can include the notes E♯ or B♯ (or both). If you play E♯ (the note a half-step above E) on the piano, you're actually playing F. In the same way, playing B♯ is equivalent to playing C.

# Chapter 4: Modes

Now that you have an understanding of the function of Key Signatures, let's take a look at the modes. Modes are, in a sense, sub-scales of the Major scale. By numbering the notes in the Major scale, and creating a new scale on each numbered scale step of the Major scale, you will create six additional new scales (using only the notes of the original Major scale). These new sub-scales are known as **Modes**. Knowing modes thoroughly will enable you to play better basslines. Keep in mind that later, we'll be building seven chords on the scale steps of the Major scale. The modes you learn here will match up with each of these chords. This concept is important when playing improvisational music like jazz, blues, and rock & roll.

We will start with modes in the key of C Major. When learning about the patterns found throughout music, the key of C Major is the usual starting point because C Major contains only "natural" notes. However, it is important to understand that modes exist in every key. This chapter explains the process of deriving sub-scales (modes) from the numbered scales steps of the Major scale. While the examples here are limited to the key of C Major, you should be aware that every key has seven modes.

After we review the modes in the key of C Major, you will learn a pattern that is designed specifically for bassists. This pattern, which we'll call the "Super Scale", contains icons that act as substitutes for the half step/whole step patterns that occur on the bass fingerboard when extending the Major scale and its modes across all four strings and all octaves of the bass. The Super Scale pattern does not contain note names. Its sole purpose is to enable you, the four-string bassist, to project in your mind's eye the diatonic patterns of any given key center onto your fingerboard. In other words, the Super Scale is a pattern you "super-impose" on your bass fingerboard. There are several benefits to this technique. For one, the Super Scale pattern encompasses all the modes, and since it has no notes, you can apply the pattern to any given key center, so you won't need to learn all the modes in all the keys. You should still learn the half step/whole step pattern of the individual modes on the bass fingerboard, but the Super Scale allows you to see beyond individual modes. Another benefit to learning the Super Scale pattern is the ability it will give you to see the patterns of any given key center in your mind's eye before you choose the notes you intend to play when improvising, or making up what you play as you play it. Improvisation is usually considered the territory of advanced musicians since it requires not only the ability to play an instrument well, but an understanding of how modes and chords match up in any key center. In other words, musical improvisation requires a solid understanding of Diatonic Harmony. The Super Scale reveals the diatonic pattern of all notes (in any key) on the bass fingerboard. Admittedly, while no musician sticks strictly to playing only diatonic notes, knowledge of this diatonic pattern is a solid starting point for any student of musical improvisation.

The use of the modes in music can be traced back to Ancient Greece. Because of this, each of the seven modes bears a name that sounds very much like it came from Ancient Greece. While these names may sound silly at first, it's a good idea to learn each mode name (and the associated whole step/half step pattern of each mode) so that when working with other musicians who know the modes, you can communicate without sounding like you're speaking Greek.

Here is the C Major scale and its modes:

**Ionian** - Otherwise known as the Major Scale. The Ionian mode has a Do-Re-Mi feel to it. This is a "Major" type mode as determined by the 1st, 3rd, and 5th notes of the mode. (You'll learn more about Major and Minor when we study chords later in this book.)

**Dorian** - The Dorian mode is a Minor type mode. It's great for funk basslines and is a favorite of jazz saxophone players, who love to "stretch out" on modal tunes.

**Phrygian** - The Phrygian mode is a Minor type mode. This mode has a distinctive Spanish Gypsy sound.

**Lydian** - The Lydian mode is a Major type mode. This mode can be a bit difficult to use because the interval from the root (or first scale tone of this mode) to the fourth scale tone is a Tritone. Because of this Tritone, the Lydian Mode always seems to want to resolve to a different mode. (We'll learn more about the Tritone later.)

**Mixolydian** - The Mixolydian mode is a Dominant type mode. (You'll learn more about the term "Dominant" when we study chords later in this book.) This mode is used widely by bassists when playing blues and jazz "walking" bass lines.

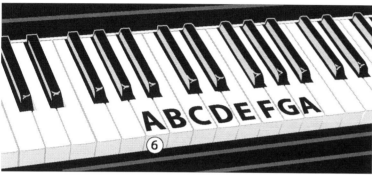

**Aeolian** - The Aeolian mode is a Minor type mode. The Aeolian mode is also referred to as the "Natural Minor" scale or the "Relative Minor" scale.

**Locrian** -   The Locrian mode is a Diminished type mode. (You'll also learn more about the term "Diminished" when we study chords later on.) As with the Lydian mode, this mode can also be difficult to use because the interval from the root (or first scale tone of this mode) to the fifth scale tone is a Tritone (3 whole steps).

The concept here is that if you build a sub-scale on each of the 7 steps of the Major scale, you will have 7 modes. The quality (or type) of these modes can be classified as Major, Minor, Dominant or Diminished. (We'll learn about "quality" when we study chords. For now, see table below:)

| Scale Step | Mode Name | Mode Quality (or Mode type) |
| --- | --- | --- |
| 1 | Ionian *(same as the Major Scale)* | Major |
| 2 | Dorian | Minor |
| 3 | Phrygian | Minor |
| 4 | Lydian | Major |
| 5 | Mixolydian | Dominant (aligns w/ Dominant 7th chord) |
| 6 | Aeolian *(same as the Natural Minor Scale)* | Minor |
| 7 | Locrian | Diminished (aligns w/ Diminished 7th chord) |

# Modes on the Bass Fingerboard

Here is what the seven modes look like on the bass fingerboard (in "Root Position"):

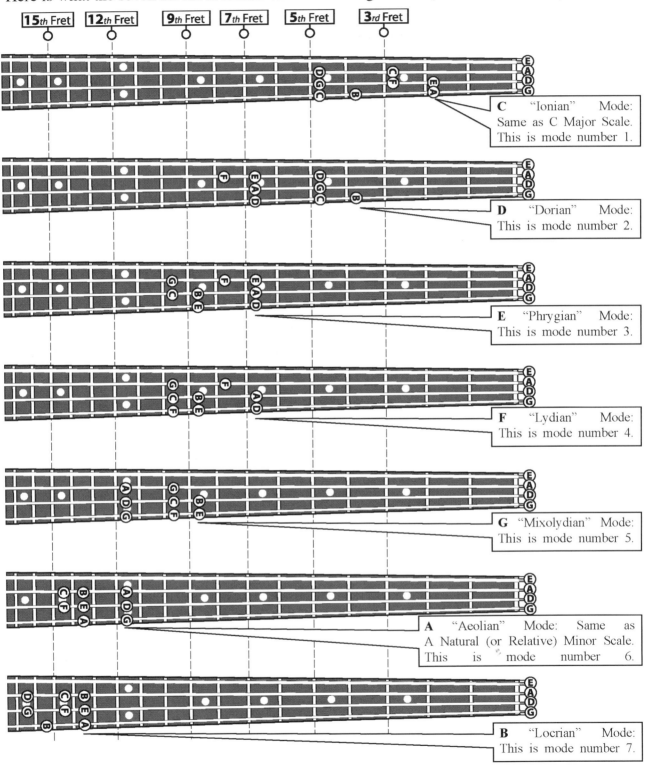

# The "Super Scale"

So, now that you've endured all the professorial jargon that's required to fully understand the value of the Diatonic Harmony system, you're ready for the most powerful scale you'll ever learn - the Super Scale! Really, it should be called the "Master Pattern", because it's a pattern that you'll memorize. However, since this "master pattern" encompasses ALL the modes on all four strings of the 4 string bass, we'll call it the Super Scale because it will change the way you view the bass fingerboard. This Super Scale pattern has 2 distinct parts, as you will see.

For the purpose of simplification and visualization, we're going to convert whole steps and half steps into symbols that we can see. Keeping in mind that 2 half steps are equal to one whole step, we'll use household items to help us visualize this. So let's pretend that a half step is a staple (from a common stapler) and a whole step is a paper clip. As you can see in the illustration below, 2 staples are the same size as 1 paper clip (just as 2 half steps add up to one whole step.)

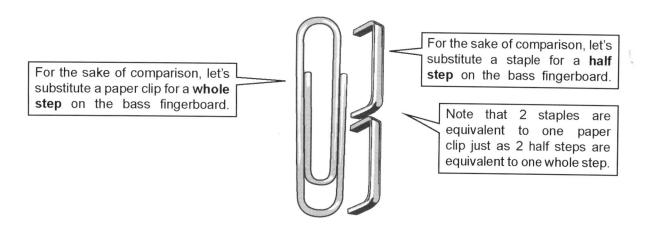

Let's take a look at these substitutes next to their counterpart on the bass fingerboard:

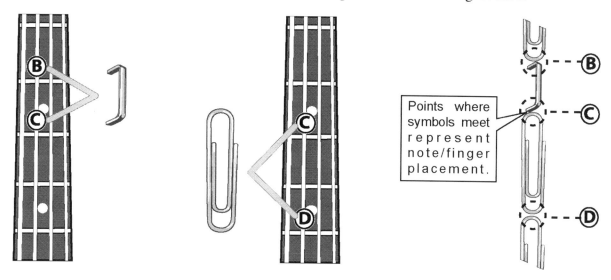

So why use paper clips and staples? One reason only: to reveal the pattern that is the Super Scale!!

Chapter 4 - Modes - The "Super Scale"   35

# Analyzing the Super Scale

As mentioned previously, the Super Scale has two distinct parts. Separating the Super Scale pattern into two parts enables us to see specific features of each part that will make the whole pattern easier to memorize. The illustration below identifies these 2 parts of the master pattern.

> The pattern shown here is a substitute for the pattern of Diatonic notes on the bass fingerboard in any key. Diatonic notes are the notes contained within a Major Scale and its associated modes. No note names are included here because no matter what key you're in, this pattern is always consistent and the pattern can be shifted as needed. Mastering this pattern will enable you to visualize the Diatonic notes on the bass fingerboard regardless of the key center. You can play the notes in this pattern in any order you choose.

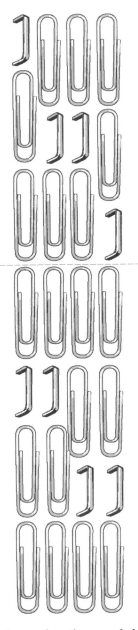

> Notice the dividing line that separates the pattern into two distinct halves. In the next example, we'll be taking a close look at each of these halves.

If you look at the separate halves, you might notice that each half contains a separate pattern, and even if you spin each half of the pattern upside down by rotating it clockwise, it retains the same whole step and half step pattern. By breaking down the pattern and learning each half separately, you can more easily learn the entire pattern. Learning both halves of the pattern will go a long way toward mastery of the Diatonic notes on the bass fingerboard.

Let's look at the top half of the pattern shown on the previous page. (The half of the pattern *above* the dividing line.) You'll notice that the half step and whole step patterns are identical, even when the pattern above the dividing line is flipped upside-down by rotating clockwise:

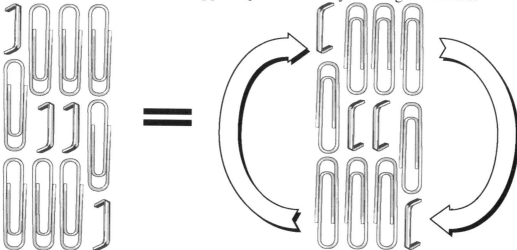

The same holds true for the lower half of the pattern (below the dividing line) shown on the previous page. The half step and whole step patterns are identical, even when the pattern below the dividing line is flipped upside-down by rotating clockwise:

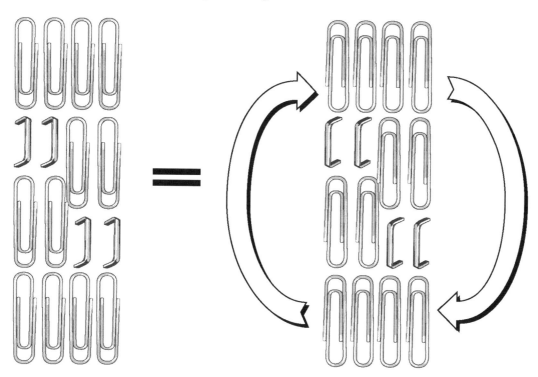

Next, we'll look at the way these two patterns alternate. Be aware that depending on what you are playing, the pattern initially pictured on top might actually be the lower half of the pattern and vice-versa.

The illustration below shows how the two halves of the pattern alternate (regardless of which half is on top):

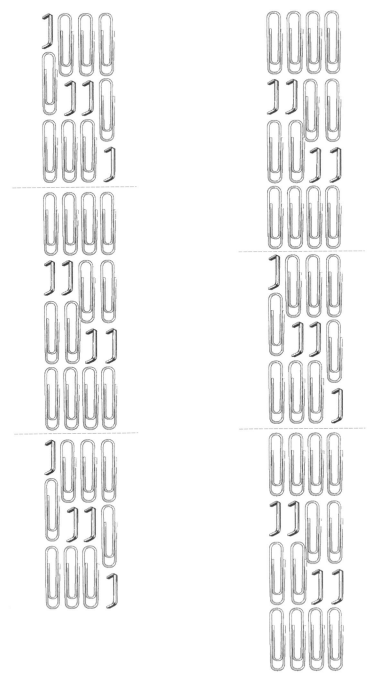

When it comes right down to it, the fingerboard is the heart of the bass. As simplified as this staple and paper clip pattern may seem, the goal in removing all the notes, and replacing them with a pattern is to simplify the process of knowing scales and modes on your fingerboard. It is quite common in the study of music theory to seek patterns that can be applied across any key. Hopefully, when you visualize the Super Scale pattern atop your bass fingerboard, you will see the underlying Diatonic patterns on the bass fingerboard more clearly and completely in any key.

In addition to enabling you to visualize the master pattern across all four strings of the bass, it is possible to use the staple/paper clip comparison to see the patterns that emerge on one and then two strings. Take a look at the examples below and play the one string and two string patterns on your bass. Playing all of these 1, 2, and 4 string patterns will help you to commit them to memory.

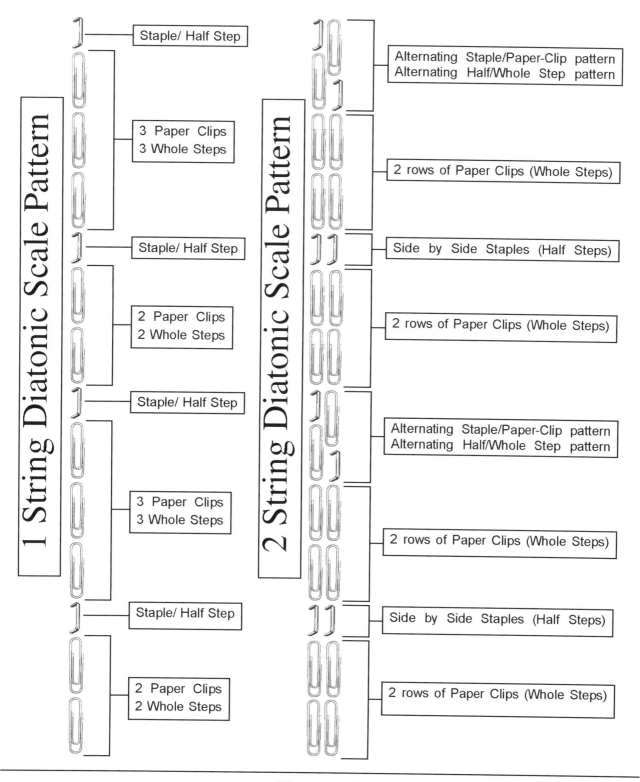

Chapter 4 - Modes - Analyzing the Super Scale

# Positions of all modes within the Super Scale

As mentioned, the Super Scale pattern encompasses all seven of the modes in any key. The following diagrams show the position of each of the seven modes within the Super Scale pattern. The notes names are left out of the diagrams below because these patterns are consistent regardless of the key center. The root position pattern of each mode is represented by the dark pattern.

Major Scale (Ionian Mode) represented by the dark (accentuated) pattern:

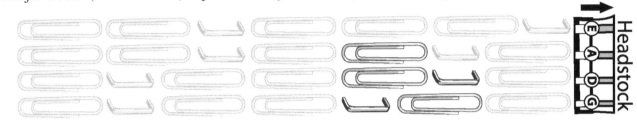

Dorian Mode:

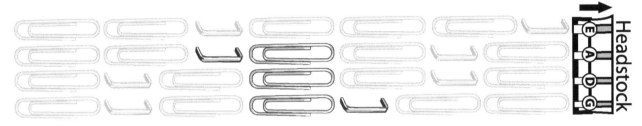

Phrygian Mode (shown in two locations within the super scale pattern):

Lydian Mode (shown in two locations within the super scale pattern):

Mixolydian Mode (shown in two locations within the super scale pattern):

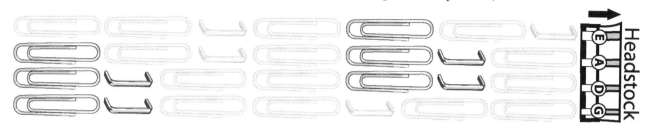

Aeolian Mode (Natural Minor Scale):

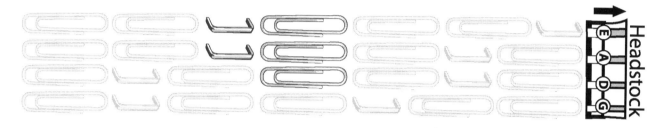

Locrian Mode:

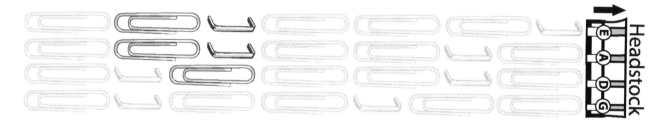

As you can see from these examples, the Super Scale pattern contains all the modes. The modes above are presented in root position, but no matter how you play the notes in any given mode, and regardless of the position you play that mode in, the half step and whole step patterns of that mode will still be present within the Super Scale pattern.

Note: See Page 34 for another look at the Modes.

# Super Scale in C Major Key Center

Let's go back to fingerboard notes revealed by the story about the friendly Grandmother, and replace the half steps and whole steps revealed by the Natural note names (no sharps or flats) with staples and paper clips to see the patterns that emerge:

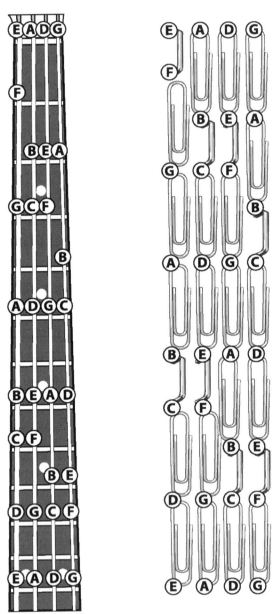

The example above represents only the key center of C Major. Be aware that the Super Scale pattern can be applied to any key by shifting the pattern as needed. In the following examples, we'll take a look at the Super Scale pattern overlaid above the bass fingerboard displaying the notes of the G Major key center, followed by the F Major key center. Again, the sole purpose of the Super Scale pattern is to enable you to visualize the diatonic placement of half steps and whole steps on the bass fingerboard in any given key center.

# Super Scale in other Key Centers

As long as you are playing in a Major Key or any one of the related modes, the patterns in the Super Scale remain consistent. Take a look at the illustrations below and note the dividing line between the patterns. Although these examples are in different keys, and therefore the overall position of the pattern has shifted, each half of the pattern remains intact.

The Super Scale example below shows a G Major key center (the G Major scale and associated modes) overlaid above the Super Scale pattern. *(Note the dividing line)*

The Super Scale example below shows an F Major key center (the F Major scale and associated modes) overlaid above the Super Scale pattern. *(Note that the missing elements in the upper half of the pattern appear after the lower half, under the dividing line.)*

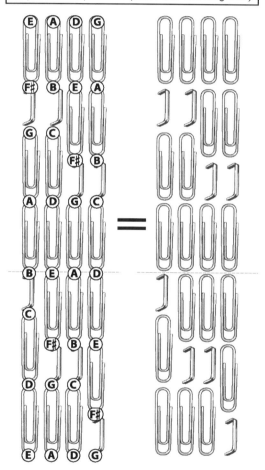
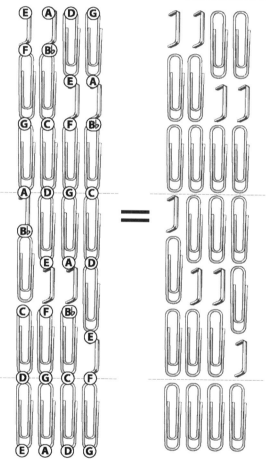

Mastering the Super Scale pattern should make it much easier to visually see the positions of all the notes that are available on the bass fingerboard in any given key center. When you can see this pattern in your mind (overlaid on your fingerboard) you can more clearly see the Diatonic patterns up and down the bass fingerboard, and therefore utilize your 4 string bass to it's fullest potential. Also, all seven modes are contained in this pattern, so learning to apply the Super Scale in any key will make it unnecessary to learn all of the modes in all of the keys. Again, you should still learn the half step/whole step pattern of the individual modes on the bass fingerboard, but the Super Scale allows you to see beyond individual modes.

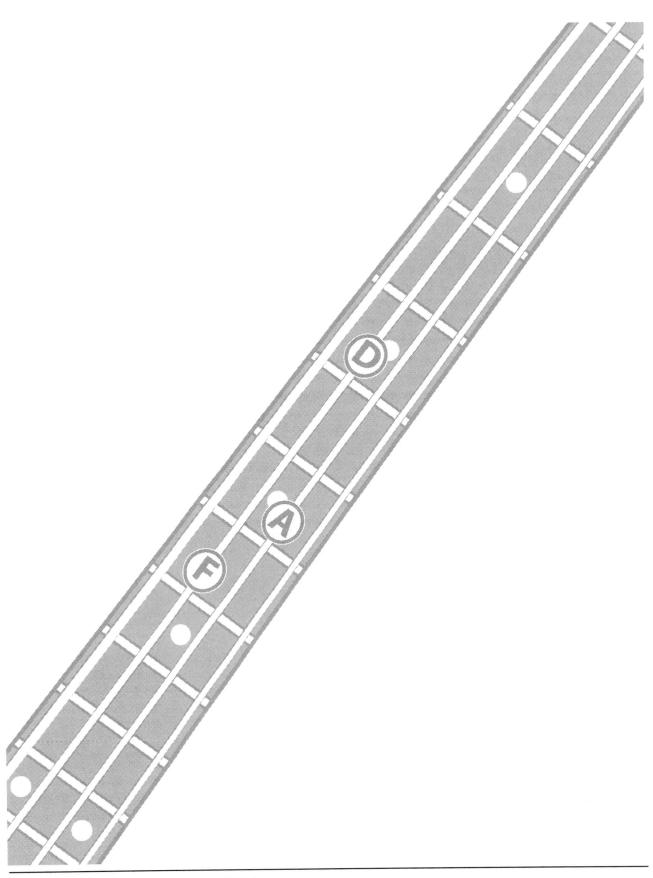

# Chapter 5: Seconds & Thirds as Intervals

Whole steps and half steps are musical building blocks. In this lesson, we'll reclassify Whole Steps and Half Steps as "Intervals". An Interval is basically the distance between one note and another. We'll start with the most basic intervals - the Minor Second and the Major Second. You already know these intervals as the Half Step and the Whole Step. Once we have a solid understanding of Seconds, we'll use Seconds to construct Thirds. Thirds - the Minor Third and Major Third - are the intervals which are used as building blocks for Chords. Chord knowledge is essential to understanding Harmony, which is the next level in understanding music. Harmony is the simultaneous sounding of at least several notes. Examples of harmony can be seen in a strummed guitar chord, a choir, or a pianist playing chords. While bassists aren't expected to play chords, they are expected to play basslines to accompany instruments that are capable of playing chords. So if you plan to play the correct notes when playing along with chords, you should understand chord construction, or the elements of harmony. But before you can do that, you must understand Seconds and Thirds as Intervals.

### Let's start with the basics.

It's time for the half step and whole step to graduate. While the half step and whole step are the basic building blocks of all Western music, they need to graduate to the next level in order to enable us to see and analyze the big picture of music. Intervals provide that graduation. Here's one definition of an interval as it applies to music:

*An interval represents a movement from one named note to another differently named note (a melodic interval) or the simultaneous sounding of two differently named notes (a harmonic interval). Melodic interval movement can be upward or downward. Harmonic intervals can also be analyzed from the upper note to the lower note and vice-versa.*

In the same way the basic building blocks of music are the whole step and half step, the basic building blocks of intervals are the Minor Second (defined as a half step between one note name and another note name) and the Major Second (defined as a whole step between one note name and another note name). So as you can see, referring to the half step as a Minor Second, and the whole step as a Major Second *is* the graduation ceremony for the half step and whole step. From now on, when referring to *intervals*, these two building blocks - the whole step and the half step - will be known as the Minor Second and the Major Second. As we move forward, you'll see how these Seconds as intervals are combined to create Thirds, which are then combined to create chords. While knowledge of scales enhances your ability to create melodies, knowledge of chords will enhance your ability to understand and create harmonies. The starting point for learning chords is the stacking of Seconds to form the interval of a Third. The Third is the interval that is the basic building block for creating chords. Before we move on to Thirds, let's make sure we have a solid understanding of Seconds as intervals.

**Examples of Seconds:** As mentioned before, an Interval involves two notes with different names. So, even though moving from C to C♯ on the keyboard is in fact a half step, it is not a Minor Second interval because there is only one note name – C. (C♯ is still a variant of C.) However, if we move from C to D♭, we are moving a Minor Second because there are 2 note names (hence the term "Second") – C and D(flat). Yes it sounds the same when you go from C to C♯ as it does when you go from C to D♭, and C♯ and D♭ are the same black key on the piano keyboard, but, for the purpose of learning music theory, the interval of a second requires two different notes names.

Similarly, moving from D♭ to D♯ is a whole step, but in order for this interval to be considered a Major Second, we'd need to move from D♭ to E♭ - a whole step with 2 note names - D and E.

## Constructing Thirds:

The term "Third" derives its name from the 3 notes it encompasses. Just as a Second contains 2 note names, a Third spans 3 note names. There are two types of thirds – the Major Third and the Minor Third. Here's the method for constructing thirds:

**Constructing a Minor Third** - A Minor Third is constructed by combining a Major Second and a Minor Second spanning 3 note names. That's the quick definition.

Here's more detail – starting with the note **D** on the piano keyboard, move up a whole step to **E**.

> The Interval (distance) between D and E is a Whole Step, referred to as a Major Second.

By doing this, we've created an interval of a Major Second – D and E are the 2 note names, and they are separated by a whole step.

Continuing, if we play an **E** on the piano keyboard, and move up a half step to **F**, we've created an interval of a Minor Second – E and F are the 2 note names, and they are separated by a half step (or Minor Second).

> The Interval (distance) between E and F is a Half Step, referred to as a Minor Second.

Keep in mind that in order to create an interval of a Third (Major or Minor), we need 3 note names.

If we combine the previous examples in order to create the interval of a Third (2 different notes spanning 3 note names), we can see from the Second intervals contained between the notes that D and F are separated by a Major Second and a Minor Second – D to E and E to F.

The Interval (distance) between D and F is equal to a Whole Step (Major Second) plus a Half Step (Minor Second). Because this interval encompasses 3 note names, it is considered a Third. Also, since the interval is composed of a Major Second and a Minor Second, it is considered a Minor Third.

The interval from D to F is considered a **Minor Third**, which is constructed by combining a Major Second and a Minor Second spanning 3 note names. It doesn't matter whether the Minor Second is on the top or the bottom of the equation, as long as the Minor Third contains a Minor Second and a Major Second.

To further illustrate this, let's start on the note B on the piano keyboard and move up a half step to C. By doing this, we've created a Minor Second – B and C are the 2 note names, and they are separated by a half step. Continuing, if we play a C on the piano keyboard, and move up a whole step to D, we've created Major Second – C and D are the 2 note names, and they are separated by a whole step.

The Interval (distance) between B and D is equal to a Half Step (Minor Second) plus a Whole Step (Major Second). Because this interval encompasses 3 note names, it is considered a Third. Also, since the interval is composed of a Minor Second and a Major Second, it is considered a Minor Third.

Looking at these notes in the context of a Third – if we play the notes B and D, we can see from the Second intervals contained between these notes that B and D are separated by the intervals of a Minor Second and a Major Second – B to C and C to D. This makes B to D a Minor Third.

**So, the rule for constructing a Minor Third is:**

> Major Second + Minor Second = Minor Third
> – or –
> Minor Second + Major Second = Minor Third

Keep in mind that the first and last notes of this formula encompass 3 note names, but the underlying intervals between those note names are the Major and the Minor Second.

**Constructing a Major Third** – A Major Third is constructed by combining two Major Seconds spanning 3 note names. That's the quick definition.

Here's more detail – starting with the note F on the piano keyboard, move up a whole step to G.

The Interval (distance) between F and G is a Whole Step, referred to as a Major Second.

By doing this, we've created a Major Second – F and G are the 2 note names, and they are separated by a whole step. Continuing, play the note G on the piano keyboard, and move up a whole step to A.

The Interval (distance) between G and A is also a Whole Step, referred to as a Major Second.

By moving from G to A, we've created another Major Second – G and A are the 2 note names, and they are separated by a whole step.

Now, regarding our mission to create a Major Third; if we play the notes F and A, we can see from the Second intervals contained between these notes that F and A are separated by two Major Seconds – F to G and G to A. This makes the interval between F and A a Major Third, since moving from F to A encompasses 3 note names - F, G, and A.

The Interval (distance) between F and A is equal to a Whole Step (Major Second) plus another Whole Step (Major Second). Because this interval encompasses 3 note names, it is considered a Third. Also, since the interval is composed of a Major Second and another Major Second, it is considered a Major Third.

## So, the rule for constructing a Major Third is:

### Major Second + Major Second = Major Third

Again, the first and last notes of this formula encompass 3 note names, but the underlying intervals between those note names are the two Major Seconds.

Chapter 5 - Seconds and Thirds

# Major and Minor Thirds on the Bass Fingerboard

Let's take another look at Major and Minor Thirds from the perspective of the bass fingerboard. We'll start by analyzing the intervals between notes D and F. The illustration below shows the distance between D and E on the bass fingerboard:

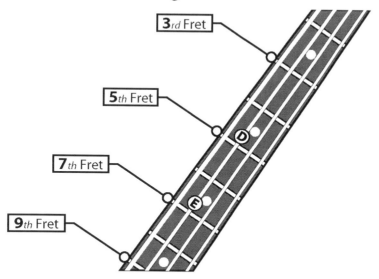

As you can see, the distance from D to E is a whole step, otherwise referred to as a Major Second.

Now let's take a look at the interval between E and F (below.)

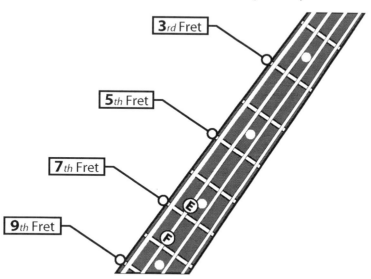

The illustration above shows that the distance from E to F is a half step, otherwise referred to as a Minor Second.

Next we'll analyze the Interval between D and F on the bass fingerboard. By combining the previous examples of Second intervals in order to create the interval of a Third (2 different notes spanning 3 note names), we can see that D and F are separated by a Major Second and a Minor Second – D to E and E to F. This creates an Interval of a Minor Third. As you can see in the illustration below, D and F are separated by the distance of a Major Second (Whole Step) and a Minor Second (Half Step).

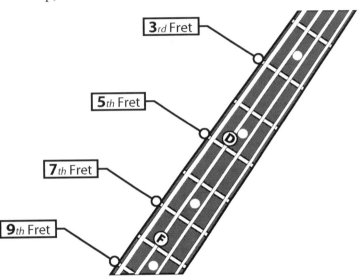

As is usually the case with the bass, there is more than one way to play a given interval. The illustration below shows another way to play a Minor Third using the same notes - D to F:

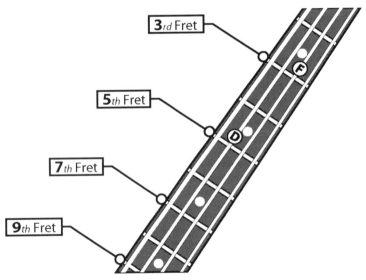

So be aware of what a Minor Third looks like on the bass, and be aware that there are two ways to "spell out" this interval on the bass fingerboard.

Now let's use the intervals between C and E to review the Major Third on the bass fingerboard. The illustration below shows the distance between C and D on the bass fingerboard:

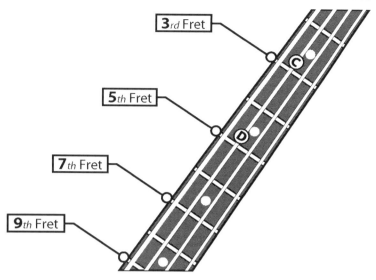

As you can see, the distance from C to D is a whole step, otherwise referred to as a Major Second.

Now let's take a look at the interval between D and E (below.)

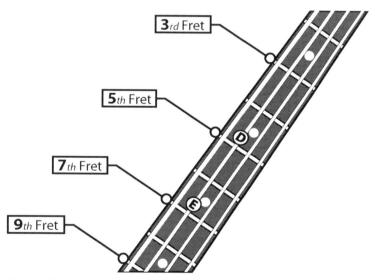

The illustration above shows that the distance from D to E is also a whole step, or Major Second.

Next we'll analyze the Interval between C and E on the bass fingerboard. By combining the previous examples of Second intervals in order to create the interval of a Third (2 different notes spanning 3 note names), we can see that C and E are separated by a Major Second and another Major Second – C to D and D to E. This creates an Interval of a Major Third.

The following illustrations show two different ways to play a Major Third on the bass fingerboard.

Example 1 - C and E notes a Major Third apart on the same string:

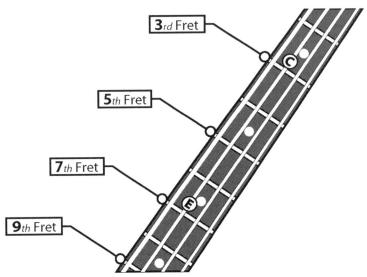

Example 2 - C and E notes a Major Third apart on 2 (adjacent) strings:

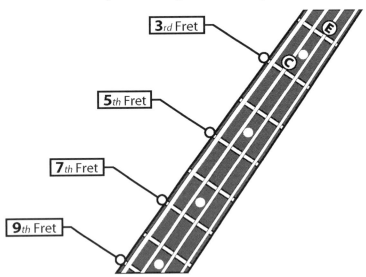

## Major and Minor Quality

As we go forward, be aware of the term *Quality*. Quality, as used when referring to chords or intervals, refers to whether those *intervals* are qualified as Major or Minor, and whether the specified *chords* are qualified as Major, Minor, or Diminished. So far we've learned about Major and Minor Thirds. What you should understand from this lesson is that Thirds come in two types, or two qualities - Major and Minor. This will become important when learning Triads, which are 3 note chords constructed from Thirds.

Chapter 5 - Seconds and Thirds

# Chapter 6: Triads

The most basic form of a chord is the Triad. Triads are 3 note chords which are built upon the first (also referred to as the *root* of the chord), third, and fifth notes of the underlying scale or mode (on each of the seven steps of the underlying Major scale). Triads are also constructed from combinations of Major and/or Minor Thirds, which are the basic interval units used to create chords. Why does a bassist need to know chords? Because in order to play along with the guitarist, keyboardist, and others, and play the correct notes (and rather than just playing only the root note of each chord) the bassist must understand chords. When learning triads, it's important to understand the "Quality" of the Triad. *Quality* refers to whether the Triad is Major, Minor, or Diminished. In order to determine Triad Quality, you will need to learn how to construct triads.

## About Triads:

Triads are 3 note chords which are built upon the first, third, and fifth notes of the underlying scale or mode. Because they use notes 1, 3, and 5 of the underlying scale, the basic component of triads is the Major and/or Minor Third. Remember, understanding chords requires an understanding of Thirds, both Major and Minor. Triads utilize the tones/notes on scale steps 1, 3, and 5 - basically every other note in the scale (up to the fifth note). Each of the notes in a Triad is a Third apart.

There are 3 basic types of triads - Major, Minor, Diminished. A fourth type, the Augmented Triad does not occur naturally in the Diatonic Harmony scheme. In other words, if you create triads using only the notes that exist in any given Major scale, the Augmented Triad will not occur. For that reason, we will cover the Augmented Triad as an academic exercise. The following lesson will show you the basics of constructing each type of triad.

## Constructing Triads

Let's start with the **Major Triad**. The Major Triad is composed of a Major Third on the bottom half (or "base") of the triad, and a Minor Third on the top half of the triad.

### Major Third + Minor Third = Major Triad

See the illustration below for a closer look:

In the example shown here, we see three notes. The notes on the bottom half of the triad (the lower notes - F and A) are separated by the interval of a Major Third. If you recall from the previous chapter, a Major Third is a combination of 2 Major Seconds. The notes on the top half of the triad (the higher notes - A and C) are separated by the interval of a Minor Third. Recall that a Minor Third is a combination of a Major Second and a Minor Second.

As you can see in this example, the interval from F to A is a Major Third, and the interval from A to C is a Minor Third. This makes the example shown here a **Major Triad**. It's important to note that the Major Third is at the base of this triad, while the Minor third sits above. When the bottom part of the triad is a Major Third, and the top half is a Minor Third, the *quality* of the triad is **Major**.

Next we'll look at the **Minor Triad**. The Minor Triad is composed of a Minor Third on the bottom half (or "base") of the triad, and a Major Third on the top half of the triad.

## Minor Third + Major Third = Minor Triad

See the illustration below for a closer look:

In the example shown here, we see three notes. The notes on the bottom half of the triad (the lower notes - D and F) are separated by the interval of a Minor Third. If you recall from the previous chapter, a Minor Third is a combination of a Major Second and a Minor Second. The notes on the top half of the triad (the higher notes - F and A) are separated by the interval of a Major Third. Recall that a Major Third is a combination of two Major Seconds.

The interval between D to F is a Minor Third and the interval between F to A is a Major Third. This makes the example shown here a **Minor Triad**. It's important to note that the Minor Third is at the base of this triad, while the Major Third sits above. When the bottom part of the triad is a Minor Third, and the top half is a Major Third, the quality of the triad is **Minor**.

Now let's look at the **Diminished Triad**. The Diminished Triad is composed of a Minor Third on the bottom half of the triad, and a Minor Third on the top half of the triad.

## Minor Third + Minor Third = Diminished Triad

See the illustration below for a closer look:

In the example shown here, we see three notes that are all separated by the interval of a Minor Third. These notes are B to D, and D to F. If you recall from the previous chapter, a Minor Third is a combination of a Major Second and a Minor Second.

The interval between B to D is a Minor Third and the interval between D to F is a Minor Third. This makes the example shown here a **Diminished Triad**. Note that an interval of a Minor Third occurs on both halves of the triad. When the bottom part of the triad is a Minor Third, and the top half is also a Minor Third, the quality of the triad is **Diminished**.

Last, we'll take a look at the **Augmented Triad**. The Augmented Triad is composed of a Major Third on the bottom half of the triad, and a Major Third on the top half of the triad.

The rule for the Augmented Triad is:

## Major Third + Major Third = Augmented Triad

See the illustration below for a closer look:

In the example shown here, we see three notes. The notes on the bottom half of the triad (the lower notes - F and A) are separated by the interval of a Major Third. If you recall from the previous chapter, a Major Third is a combination of 2 Major Seconds. The notes on the top half of the triad are also separated by the interval of a Major Third.

(Notes F and A are separated by a Major Third as are notes A and C#)

As you can see, in this example, the interval from F to A is a Major Third, and the interval from A to C# is also a Major Third. This makes the example shown here an **Augmented Triad**. It's important to note that there is a Major Third on both sides of this triad. When the bottom part of the triad is a Major Third, and the top half is also a Major Third, the quality of the triad is **Augmented**.

The Augmented Triad does not naturally occur in diatonic harmony because it requires tones outside of the key center, (which is why we added C# to the equation) so don't worry too much about it at this point. Just be aware of its existence – kind of like Bigfoot. Notice that C# *follows* F# in the order of sharps, so if the C is sharp, the F should be sharp. That's why the Augmented Triad doesn't exist in diatonic harmony. (But don't let that stop you from using an augmented triad if it sounds good!)

Of course, now we have to translate this triad knowledge onto the bass fingerboard. And in keeping with one of the principles of music theory, we'll look for patterns as we explore triads on the bass fingerboard.

# Triads as Arpeggios on the Bass Fingerboard

As you just learned, Triads are 3 note chords. The 3 notes contain two intervals in combination - Minor Thirds and Major Thirds. Therefore, before we start, let's review the basic building blocks of triads - Minor Thirds and Major Thirds - as they look on the bass fingerboard. Also, be aware that triads, when played on the bass, are called "arpeggios". An arpeggio is a chord played melodically, one note at a time, as opposed to a chord which is played harmonically, with all notes sounding simultaneously.

**Minor Thirds on the Bass Fingerboard**:

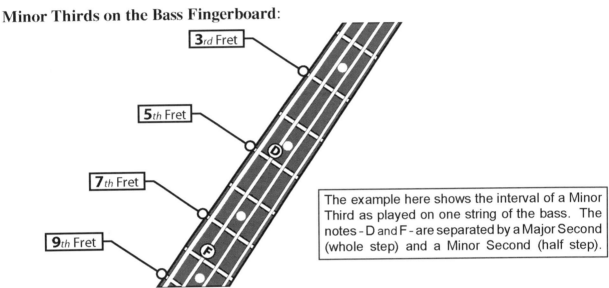

The example here shows the interval of a Minor Third as played on one string of the bass. The notes - D and F - are separated by a Major Second (whole step) and a Minor Second (half step).

As is usually the case with the bass, there is more than one way to play a given interval. The illustration below shows a way to play a Minor Third on 2 adjacent strings using the same notes - D and F.

This example shows the interval of a Minor Third as played on two strings of the bass. The notes - D and F - are still separated by a Major Second (whole step) and a Minor Second (half step), but the two notes are on adjacent strings, so these intervals are not as immediately recognizable as when the notes are on the same string. In any case, this is still a Minor Third.

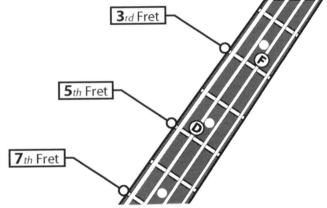

So be aware that there are two ways to "spell out" the Minor Third on the bass fingerboard: both notes on 1 string, or each note played on 2 adjacent strings. Memorize these two shapes because we will build on this knowledge as you learn to include chord tones in your bass lines. These shapes remain consistent no matter what key you're playing in. This is one advantage that the bass has over the keyboard, where a Minor Third could use any combination of black and white keys, and therefore take on any number of shapes.

## Major Thirds on the Bass Fingerboard:

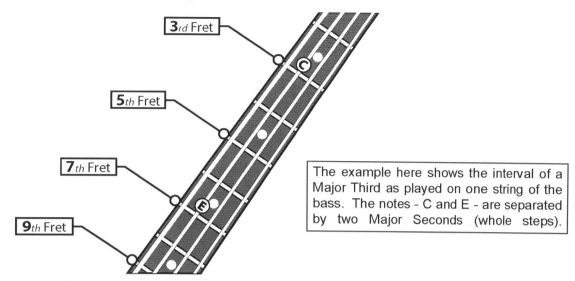

Example 2 - C and E notes a Major Third apart on 2 strings

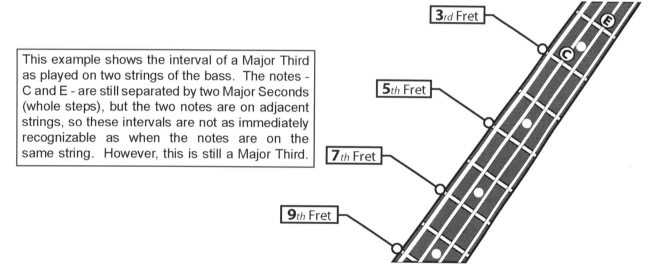

Again, be aware that there are two ways to "spell out" the Major Third on the bass fingerboard: both notes on 1 string, or each note played on 2 adjacent strings. Memorize these two shapes because we will build on this knowledge as you learn to include chord tones in your bass lines. Remember, these shapes remain consistent no matter what key you're playing in.

## Combining Major and Minor Thirds as Triads on the Fingerboard

Next, we'll take a look at triads on the bass fingerboard. As you know, Triads are 3 note chords that contain two intervals in combination - Minor Thirds and/or Major Thirds. Therefore, we're going to take the interval shapes that we just reviewed and combine them on the bass fingerboard to see some of the ways you can play triads on the bass. Keep in mind, bassists generally don't play triads as harmonic chords, with all 3 notes of the triad sounding simultaneously, but the bassist will normally incorporate arpeggiated triad notes into their basslines.

**Building Triads on the Bass Fingerboard**

By combining the Major and Minor Thirds that we just reviewed to create Triads on the bass fingerboard, we can see several patterns emerge.

Take a look at these variations of the **Major Triad** on the bass fingerboard below:

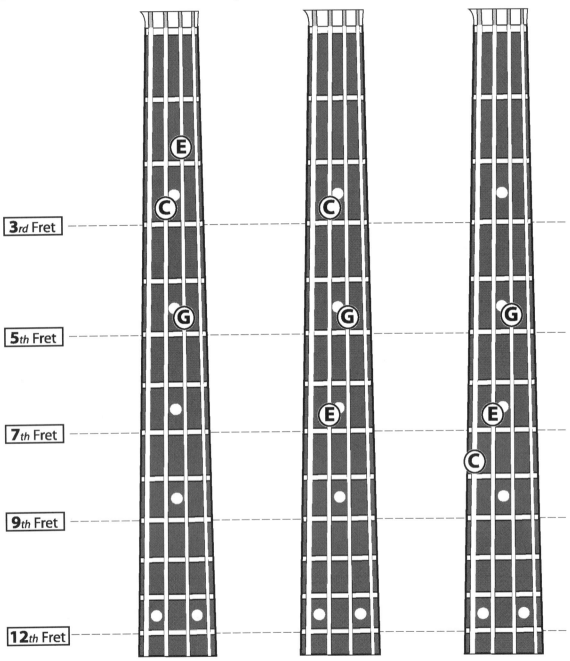

These patterns present three basic ways to play the notes contained in a C Major Triad which contains the notes C, E, and G. While you wouldn't play these particular notes simultaneously as a chord on the bass, knowing the notes of a chord will enable you to play more interesting bass lines in harmony with those instruments you accompany.

The example below shows several variations of the **Minor Triad** on the bass fingerboard:

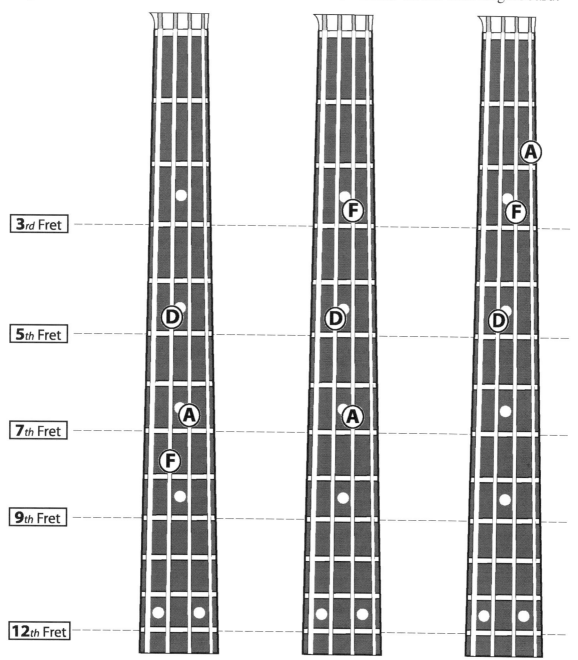

These patterns show three basic ways to play the notes contained in a D Minor Triad which contains the notes D, F, and A. Again, you wouldn't play these particular notes simultaneously as a chord on the bass, but knowing the notes of a chord will enable you to play more interesting bass lines.

Next we'll take a look at the Diminished Triad. In the next chapter, we will see the pattens that emerge when we look closely at the seven chords that are built from each note of the Major Scale. Of these seven chords, the Diminished Chord occurs only once.

The example below shows several variations of the **Diminished Triad** on the bass fingerboard:

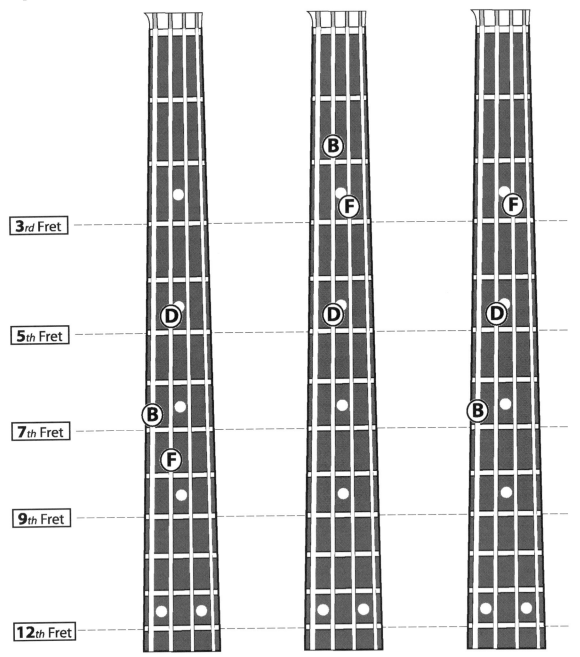

The patterns above show three basic ways to play the notes contained in a B Diminished Triad which contains the notes B, D, and F. Again, you wouldn't play these particular notes simultaneously as a chord on the bass, but knowing the notes of the chord will enable you to play more interesting bass lines.

Memorizing the shapes of the Major, Minor, and Diminished Triads on the bass fingerboard will enable you to quickly recall these chords as arpeggios in different playing situations. You should also memorize the locations of all the notes on the fingerboard and use these patterns as a way to enhance your knowledge of the note locations on the bass fingerboard, and not as a substitute for knowledge of notes on the bass fingerboard.

It is critical for you to be aware that a Triad is built on steps 1, 3, and 5 of an underlying scale or mode. The example below illustrates this concept with the C Major Triad:

As you can see, the notes C, E, & G are also labeled with their associated scale steps, 1, 3, and 5.

All triads are three note chords based on scale steps 1, 3, and 5 of the underlying scale or mode, and the notes of a triad are separated by the intervals of a combination of Major and/or Minor Thirds.

The next chapter will provide more information on the subject of triads and their construction upon the first, third and fifth scale step of each of the seven underlying modes.

Also, since bassists usually play chords in their arpeggiated form, it's important for the serious bassist to listen to chords played harmonically (for example, on a keyboard or guitar) in order to become familiar with the sound of each type (or quality) of chord.

# Chapter 7: Diatonic Harmony

You've probably seen the term *Diatonic Harmony* mentioned in this book many times prior to this, but now, it's time to explain exactly what Diatonic Harmony means.

## What is Diatonic Harmony?

As you've probably noticed, this book is about how bassists can benefit from knowing the patterns that emerge when you take a Major Scale and extend it beyond the seven notes of the scale by creating Modes and Chords from the notes in that Major Scale. And as you learned with Triads, chords can be qualified as Major, Minor, or Diminished. Diatonic Harmony is the study and analysis of music, starting with the Major Scale, and extending that Major Scale into modes (sub-scales of the Major Scale) and chords (the foundation of harmony) in order to find consistent patterns that occur in music, regardless of the Key Center. While the serious composer should definitely take college level courses in the study of Diatonic Harmony (and Music Theory), it is possible to gain a solid understanding of Diatonic Harmony by gaining knowledge of the patterns that arise when you extend the Major Scale into modes and chords. Also, be aware that using numbers rather than note names is very important to the study of Diatonic Harmony because these numbers are very useful in identifying patterns that can be applied universally to different key centers.

So, in the interest of getting to the heart of Diatonic Harmony, let's take a look at the C Major scale, and in the same way we previously built a new mode from each step in the scale, we will now build a triad for each step in the scale. After that, we'll use our knowledge of triad construction to analyze the Quality of these new triads to see what patterns emerge.

To keep things simple, we'll start again with the C Major Scale. No Sharps, No Flats, but the patterns that emerge will be the same no matter the key center. The diagram below shows the C Major Scale. Underneath the scale note names are numbers 1 through 8. (*The note assigned to number 8 is the same as the note assigned to number 1 - number 8 is referred to as the octave of number 1.*) The purpose of the numbers is to identify any patterns that can be applied to different key centers universally.

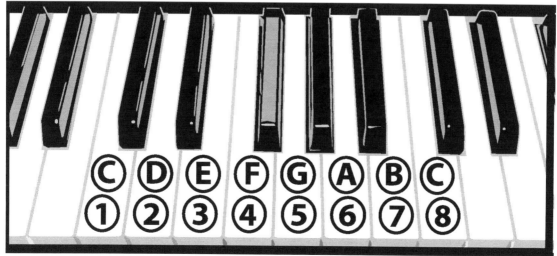

We'll now build a triad upon each of the seven scale steps. The following diagrams will contain a number with a shadow. This shadowed number will represent the scale step upon which the triad is being built. We'll start with the triad built upon the **first step** of the C Major Scale.

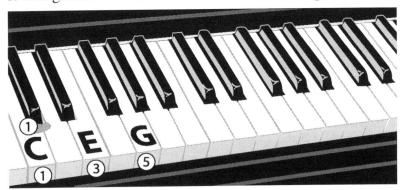

This illustration shows a Triad built upon the first scale step of the C Major Scale (as represented by the shadowed number 1.) **C** is the first note of the C Major Scale, **E** is the third note, and **G** is the fifth note. If we analyze the intervals between the notes, we see that the distance between C and E is a Major Third, and the distance between E and G is a Minor Third. Therefore, based on the parameters discussed in the previous chapter, this is a **Major Triad**. *(Major Third + Minor Third= Major Triad)*

Next we'll evaluate the triad built upon the **second step** of the C Major Scale, which is the D note.

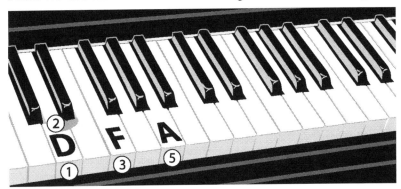

The illustration here shows a Triad built starting on the D note, which is the second scale step of the C Major scale (as represented by the shadowed number 2.) **D** is the first note of the underlying Dorian Mode, **F** is the third note, and **A** is the fifth note. If we analyze the intervals between the notes, we see that the distance between D and F is a Minor Third, and the distance between F and A is a Major Third. Therefore, based on the criteria discussed in the previous chapter, this is a **Minor Triad**. *(Minor Third + Major Third= Minor Triad)*

We'll move on to look at the Triad built on the **third step** on the C Major scale, which is E.

In this illustration, we see a Triad built starting on the E note, which is the third scale step of the C Major scale (as represented by the shadowed number 3.) **E** is the first note of the underlying Phrygian Mode, **G** is the third note, and **B** is the fifth note. If we analyze the intervals between the notes, we see that the distance between E and G is a Minor Third, and the distance between G and B is a Major Third. Based on the criteria discussed in the previous chapter, this is a **Minor Triad**. *(Minor Third + Major Third= Minor Triad)*

Continuing, let's look at the triad built upon the **fourth step** of the C Major Scale, which is F.

This illustration shows a Triad built upon the fourth scale step of the C Major Scale (as represented by the shadowed number 4.) **F** is the first note of the underlying F Lydian Mode, **A** is the third note, and **C** is the fifth note. If we analyze the intervals between the notes, we see that the distance between F and A is a Major Third, and the distance between A and C is a Minor Third. Therefore, based on what we learned in the previous chapter, this is a **Major Triad**. *(Major Third + Minor Third= Major Triad)*

Now let's look at the triad built upon the **fifth step** of the C Major Scale, which is G.

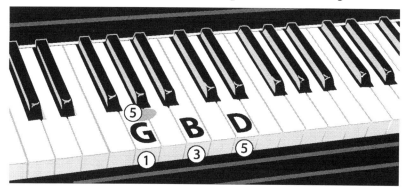

Here we see a Triad built upon the fifth scale step of the C Major Scale (as represented by the shadowed number 5.) **G** is the first note of the underlying G Mixolydian Mode, **B** is the third note, and **D** is the fifth note. If we analyze the intervals between the notes, we see that the distance between G and B is a Major Third, and the distance between B and D is a Minor Third. Therefore, based on what we've learned about triad construction, this is a **Major Triad**. *(Major Third + Minor Third= Major Triad)*

We'll now analyze the triad built upon the **sixth step** of the C Major Scale, which is A.

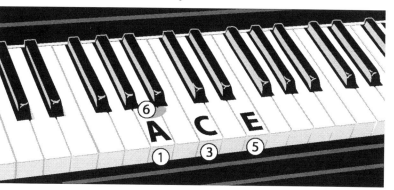

The next illustration shows a Triad built upon the sixth scale step of the C Major Scale (as represented by the shadowed number 6.) **A** is the first note of the underlying **A** Aeolian Mode, **C** is the third note, and **E** is the fifth note. If we analyze the intervals between the notes, we see that the distance between A and C is a Minor Third, and the distance between C and E is a Major Third. Therefore, based on what we've learned about triad construction, this is a **Minor Triad**. *(Minor Third + Major Third= Minor Triad)*

Finally, we'll analyze the triad built upon the **seventh step** of the C Major Scale, which is B.

The last Triad illustration shows a Triad built upon the seventh scale step of the C Major Scale (as represented by the shadowed number 7.) **B** is the first note of the underlying **B** Locrian Mode, **D** is the third note, and **F** is the fifth note. If we analyze the intervals between the notes, we see that the distance between B and D is a Minor Third, and the distance between D and F is also a Minor Third. Therefore, based on the rules of triad construction, this is a **Diminished Triad**. *(Minor Third + Minor Third= Diminished Triad)*

If you take a look at each of the triads above, and as you evaluate the quality of the chord at each numbered scale step, you will see a very important pattern. It looks like this:

The Triad at position 1 is a **Major Triad**
The Triad at position 2 is a **Minor Triad**
The Triad at position 3 is a **Minor Triad**
The Triad at position 4 is a **Major Triad**
The Triad at position 5 is a **Major Triad**
The Triad at position 6 is a **Minor Triad**
The Triad at position 7 is a **Diminished Triad**

To simplify: when constructing triads from the notes at each numbered step of a Major scale, the following pattern arises:

> 1 = Major Triad
> 2 = Minor Triad
> 3 = Minor Triad
> 4 = Major Triad
> 5 = Major Triad
> 6 = Minor Triad
> 7 = Diminished Triad

So, in this emerging pattern:

> **Triads 1, 4, and 5 are qualified as Major Triads.**
>
> **Triads 2, 3, and 6 are qualified as Minor Triads.**
>
> **Triad 7 is qualified as a Diminished Triad.**

That's it. The Diatonic Harmony scheme as it applies to triads in Major Key centers. Triads 1, 4, and 5 are *Major*, Triads 2, 3, and 6 are *Minor*, and Triad 7 is *Diminished*. Taking a Major scale and expanding it beyond just notes and into a harmonic dimension by building a chord on each scale step, resulting in a predictable pattern using numbered scale steps and knowledge of chord construction - this is the basis of much of Western music dating back centuries. Of course, creativity drives most musicians not to restrict their compositions to one scale, or one key center, but, if you ever wondered how composers decide which melodies to create and which chords to include when creating harmony to accompany their melodies, you'll find that the Diatonic Harmony scheme is often the starting point. Creativity provides infinite choices. If you're a songwriter, Diatonic Harmony serves to narrow your starting point as a creative musician from infinite choices to the focused and manageable place where you can begin. If you doubt the widespread use of diatonic harmony in Western Music, take any hymn, symphony, or top 40 hit song, and analyze the melody and harmony of that composition. Without a doubt, you will find Diatonic Harmony at work. And THAT is the reason you as a bassist and musician need to understand Diatonic Harmony.

## Relative Minor

So far we've learned about Major Scales with half steps between 3 & 4 and 7 & 8, and we've learned about Key Signatures for Major Keys. Although we've discussed modes, we only briefly discussed the fact that not all music is written in a Major key. The most widely used alternative to writing music in a Major key is to write music in a "Relative Minor" key, which is a Minor key that's "related" to a Major key – hence the term "relative minor".

For any Major Key, obtaining the Relative Minor key is as easy as shifting the Key Center to the 6th scale step of that Major scale, while keeping the Key Signature and Diatonic Harmony scheme of the Major Scale intact. Lets look more closely at that sentence. But before we do, let's define the term "Key Center". Remember the Do-Re-Mi song? If you just sing the solfa syllables of *Do, Re, Mi, Fa, Sol, La, Ti, Do*, you are singing a Major scale with the Key Center of "*Do*". If you were to shift the Key Center to the Relative Minor, which falls on the sixth scale step, in this case the "*La*" syllable, your scale will start at the "*La*" tone and the order of the solfa syllables will now be *La, Ti, Do, Re, Mi, Fa, Sol, La*. The new the key center is "*La*".

Let's look at this concept on the keyboard, using the C Major Scale as shown in the illustration below with the notes of the scale numbered 1 through 8. The lower instance of the "A" note (pictured below with a shadowed number 6 above it) represents the Relative Minor key center. In the key of C Major, if you shift to starting a scale on the **A** note, you will be playing a Natural Minor scale in the Relative Minor key. (The scale based on the Relative Minor key center is referred to as a "Natural Minor Scale".)

Shifting to the Relative Minor key center provides an alternative to composing music in a Major Key. The sixth scale step of the Major scale is the Relative Minor key center.

What you should also understand about shifting the key center to the relative minor key center, is that the Diatonic Harmony of the related Major Key is still intact. In other words, the quality of each triad built upon each scale step remains as follows:

For Major Keys:

- **1=Major**
- **2=Minor**
- **3=Minor**
- **4=Major**
- **5=Major**
- **6 = Minor**
- **7 =Diminished**

However, you as a musician should be able to shift your understanding of Diatonic Harmony regarding the Relative Minor key center. For example, when considering the chords you might use to harmonize a Natural Minor Scale (the scale/mode that occurs on the sixth step of the related Major scale – the Relative Minor step) you might want to retain the numbering system for the Diatonic Harmony scheme for Major Keys. In other words, since your key center has shifted to the sixth step of the Major Key, you could remember your Diatonic Harmony scheme by retaining the numbering for the Major Key.

Chapter 7 - Diatonic Harmony - Relative Minor

If retaining the numbering system and Diatonic relationships for the related Major Key:

For "**A**" Natural Minor – the "Relative Minor" to C Major:

- **A/6 = Minor**
- **B/ 7 =Diminished**
- **C/1=Major**
- **D/2=Minor**
- **E/3=Minor**
- **F/4=Major**
- **G/5=Major**

Or, as a general rule (which could be applied to any key):

- **6 = Minor**
- **7 =Diminished**
- **1=Major**
- **2=Minor**
- **3=Minor**
- **4=Major**
- **5=Major**

…or, you might prefer to renumber (and re-memorize) the Diatonic Harmony Scheme for a Relative Minor key using the Relative Minor note as the new key center as follows:

- **1 = Minor**
- **2 =Diminished**
- **3=Major**
- **4=Minor**
- **5=Minor**
- **6=Major**
- **7=Major**

In this example, we are not treating the Relative Minor as it relates to the Major Key center, but as if we constructed the Diatonic Harmony scheme based on the Natural Minor scale. If you do decide to shift the numbering system, you'll have more to keep track of mentally. Also, if you decide to compose a Modal piece of music, you will need to decide whether you plan to

ze the new diatonic harmony scheme as you shift your key center to the various modes.

composers would probably do well to re-memorize the Diatonic Harmony structure ...ıe Major Scale and its seven modes, but if you're learning this for the first time, it may be wisest to memorize only the diatonic harmony scheme for the Major key, and adjust the numbering system for the other modes (including the Natural Minor scale) as it relates to the numbered steps of the related Major key. Either way, these musical brain exercises will keep you busy while creating music. Let's move on.

## Roman Numerals in Musical Analysis

It is common in the study of Music Theory and Diatonic Harmony to use Roman Numerals when analyzing music. Below is a list of the Roman Numerals and the Arabic Numerals they represent.

- I = 1
- II = 2
- III = 3
- IV = 4
- V = 5
- VI = 6
- VII = 7

In advanced Music Theory, an upper case Roman Numeral represents a Major Triad, while a lower case Roman Numeral represents a Minor Triad or a Diminished Triad. Below is a list of the upper and lower case Roman Numerals as they apply to the Diatonic Harmony scheme.

- I = 1 - Major Triad
- ii = 2 - Minor Triad
- iii = 3 - Minor Triad
- IV = 4 - Major Triad
- V = 5 - Major Triad
- vi = 6 - Minor Triad
- vii° = 7 - **Diminished Triad** (a small circle to the upper-right of the **vii** is used to distingush the Diminished Triad from a Minor Triad.)

By using this numbering system, Diatonic Harmony can be used to analyze chord progressions as they apply in any key. Common chord progressions that you should learn as a beginner are the **I, IV, V** (or one, four, five) chord progression and the **ii, V, I** (two, five, one) chord progression. As you can imagine, the study of chord progressions is somewhat specialized, so for now, we'll get back to the basics.

While this all may seem very academic, understanding this information is important to the bassist who plans to work and communicate with serious musicians. And if you plan to write your own music, knowledge of Diatonic Harmony is very important.

Chapter 7 - Diatonic Harmony

# Chapter 8: Seventh Chords

The next step to understanding Diatonic Harmony is the Seventh Chord. Seventh Chords are 4 note chords made up of the first (or *root*), third, fifth, and seventh tone of a given scale/mode. Adding this fourth note (the seventh tone) to the triad modifies the basic diatonic harmony scheme by introducing a new chord type: the Dominant Seventh chord.

## About Seventh Chords

While Triads have a Quality of either Major, Minor, or Diminished, the Seventh Chord introduces the fourth chord Quality - the Dominant Seventh chord.

Seventh chords are 4 note chords which are built upon the first, third, fifth, and seventh notes of the underlying scale or mode (hence the name "Seventh Chord"). As with triads, the basic component of seventh chords are Major and Minor Thirds. Remember, understanding chords requires an understanding of Thirds, both Major and Minor. Seventh Chords utilize the tones/notes on scale steps 1, 3, 5, and 7 - basically every other note in the scale (up to the seventh note). Each of the notes in a Seventh Chord is a Third apart.

There are 4 types of seventh chords - Major, Minor, Dominant, and Diminished. The diminished seventh chord is sometimes referred to as the "half-diminished" chord, which will be explained when we cover the diminished seventh chord.

The Dominant Seventh chord holds a special place in the study of music theory. In Western Music, this Dominant Seventh chord, which is built on the fifth scale step of the underlying Major scale, provides harmonic movement because Western ears expect to hear this chord resolve, when played, to the chord based on the first step of the underlying Major scale - the Key Center.

## Constructing Seventh Chords

Let's see how these four types of chords are constructed and what factors determine their quality. We'll start with the Major Seventh Chord. The **Major Seventh chord** is constructed as follows:

> Major Third + Minor Third + Major Third
> = Major Seventh Chord

See the illustration below for a closer look:

In the example shown here, we see four notes. The notes on the bottom part, or *base* of the chord (the lower notes - C and E) are separated by the interval of a Major Third. The notes in the middle of the chord - E and G - are separated by the interval of a Minor Third. The top notes of the chord (the higher notes - G and B) are separated by the interval of a Major Third.

In the example on the previous page, the interval from C to E is a Major Third. The interval from E to G is a Minor Third. The interval from G to B is also a Major Third. Therefore, the notes C, E, G, B, combined as a seventh chord can be classified as a Major Seventh Chord.

It's important to note that a Major Third is at the base of this Seventh Chord, while a Minor Third sits in the middle, and another Major Third sits above that. When the bottom third of the Seventh Chord is a Major Third, and the middle third is a Minor Third, and the top third is a Major Third, the quality of the Seventh Chord is **Major**.

Next, we'll look at the factors that make a **Minor Seventh chord**:

> Minor Third + Major Third + Minor Third
> = Minor Seventh Chord

See the illustration below for a closer look:

In the example shown here, we see four notes. The notes on the bottom part, or *base* of the chord (the lower notes - D and F) are separated by the interval of a Minor Third. The notes in the middle of the chord - F and A - are separated by the interval of a Major Third. The top notes of the chord (the higher notes - A and C) are separated by the interval of a Minor Third.

In this example, the interval from D to F is a Minor Third, the interval from F to A is a Major Third, and the interval from A to C is a Minor Third. Therefore, the notes D, F, A, C, combined as a seventh chord can be classified as a Minor Seventh Chord. It's important to note that a Minor Third is at the base of this Seventh Chord, while a Major Third sits in the middle, and another Minor Third sits above that. When the bottom third of the Seventh Chord is a Minor Third, and the middle third is a Major Third, and the top third is a Minor Third, the quality of the Seventh Chord is **Minor**.

We'll now take a look at what makes a **Dominant Seventh chord**:

> Major Third + Minor Third + Minor Third
> = Dominant Seventh Chord

The illustration on the following page shows a seventh chord built upon G, which is the fifth scale step of the C Major scale. The notes contained in this chord are G, B, D, F. If we analyze the intervals between these notes, we'll find that the interval from G to B is a Major Third, and the interval from B to D is Minor Third, while the interval from D to F is also a Minor Third. Therefore, the notes G, B, D, and F, when combined as a seventh chord, can be classified as a Dominant Seventh Chord.

The illustration below shows a G Dominant Seventh chord:

This example shows the four notes of the G Dominant seventh chord. The notes on the bottom part, or *base* of the chord (the lower notes - G and B) are separated by the interval of a Major Third. The notes in the middle of the chord - B and D - are separated by the interval of a Minor Third. The top notes of the chord (the higher notes - D and F) are also separated by the interval of a Minor Third.

It's important to note that a Major Third is at the base of this Seventh Chord, while a Minor Third sits in the middle, and another Minor Third sits above that. When the bottom third of the Seventh Chord is a Major Third, and the middle third is a Minor Third, and the top third is a Minor Third, the quality of the Seventh Chord is **Dominant**.

Last, we'll review the construction of the **Diminished Seventh** chord:

## Minor Third + Minor Third + Major Third = Diminished Seventh Chord

See the illustration below for an example of the Diminished Seventh chord:

In the example shown here, we see four notes. The notes at the base of the chord (the lower notes - B and D) are separated by the interval of a Minor Third. The notes in the middle of the chord - D and F - are also separated by the interval of a Minor Third. The top notes of the chord (the higher notes - F and A) are separated by a Major Third.

In this example, the interval from B to D is a Minor Third, the interval from D to F is also a Minor Third, and the interval from F to A is a Major Third. Therefore, the notes B, D, F, A, when combined as a seventh chord, can be classified as a **Diminished Seventh Chord**. It's important to note that a Minor Third is at the base of this Seventh Chord, while a Minor Third sits in the middle, and a Major Third sits above that. When the bottom third of the Seventh Chord is a Minor Third, and the middle third is a Minor Third, and the top third is a Major Third, the quality of the Seventh Chord is **Diminished**.

Regarding the term *Half Diminished* - this is another name for the Diminished Seventh chord shown above. Classifying the diminished chord as "half diminished" distinguishes it from the Fully Diminished chord, which is a seventh chord composed of all Minor Third intervals. The Fully Diminished chord does not occur in Diatonic Harmony (using only the Diatonic notes of the Major Scale), so we won't cover it in this book.

# The Diatonic Pattern of Seventh Chords

Now let's analyze the diatonic pattern that occurs when we introduce the Seventh Chord. Again, we'll use the C Major scale as the key center for this exercise. We'll build Seventh Chords on each scale step and then we'll analyze the intervals between each of the notes contained in those seventh chords. When we're done, we'll look for a pattern.

The notes of the C Major scale are C, D, E, F, G, A, B, and C. To build seventh chords on each scale step of the C Major scale, we'll take each scale step and identify the notes which are an interval distance of a third, a fifth, and a seventh away from each numbered scale step note.

We'll start by building a seventh chord on Scale Step 1, which is C in this case. In the example below we see a seventh chord built in intervals of Thirds starting with **C**.

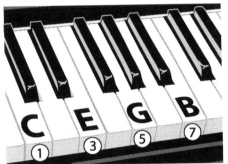

If we analyze the intervals between the notes of this four note seventh chord, we will find the following:

The interval between notes **C** and **E** is a **Major Third**
The interval between notes **E** and **G** is a **Minor Third**
The interval between notes **G** and **B** is a **Major Third**

Therefore, notes C, E, G, and B, when combined as a seventh chord, meet the criteria of a **Major Seventh Chord**. That is:

**Major Third + Minor Third + Major Third = Major Seventh Chord**

We'll continue by building a seventh chord on Scale Step 2, which is D in this case. In the example below we see a seventh chord built in intervals of Thirds starting with **D**.

If we analyze the intervals between the notes of this four note seventh chord, we will find the following:

The interval between notes **D** and **F** is a **Minor Third**
The interval between notes **F** and **A** is a **Major Third**
The interval between notes **A** and **C** is a **Minor Third**

*Note that the shadowed number 2 represents scale step 2 of the associated C Major Scale*

Therefore, notes D, F, A, and C, when combined as a seventh chord, meet the criteria of a **Minor Seventh Chord**. That is:

**Minor Third + Major Third + Minor Third = Minor Seventh Chord**

Continuing, we'll now build a seventh chord on Scale Step 3, in this case E. In the example below we see a seventh chord built in intervals of Thirds starting with **E**.

If we analyze the intervals between the notes of this four note seventh chord, we will find the following:

The interval between notes **E** and **G** is a **Minor Third**
The interval between notes **G** and **B** is a **Major Third**
The interval between notes **B** and **D** is a **Minor Third**

*Note that the shadowed number 3 represents scale step 3 of the associated C Major Scale*

Therefore, notes E, G, B, and D, when combined as a seventh chord, meet the criteria of a **Minor Seventh Chord**. That is:

| **Minor Third + Major Third + Minor Third = Minor Seventh Chord** |
|---|

Now we'll build a seventh chord on Scale Step 4, which is F in this case. In the example below we see a seventh chord built in intervals of Thirds starting with **F**.

If we analyze the intervals between the notes of this four note seventh chord, we will find the following:

The interval between notes **F** and **A** is a **Major Third**
The interval between notes **A** and **C** is a **Minor Third**
The interval between notes **C** and **E** is a **Major Third**

*Note that the shadowed number 4 represents scale step 4 of the associated C Major Scale*

Therefore, notes F, A, C, and E, when combined as a seventh chord, meet the criteria of a **Major Seventh Chord**. That is:

| **Major Third + Minor Third + Major Third = Major Seventh Chord** |
|---|

Next we'll build a seventh chord on Scale Step 5, which is G in the case of the C major scale. In the example below we see a seventh chord built in intervals of Thirds starting with **G**.

If we analyze the intervals between the notes of this four note seventh chord, we will find the following:

The interval between notes **G** and **B** is a **Major Third**
The interval between notes **B** and **D** is a **Minor Third**
The interval between notes **D** and **F** is a **Minor Third**

*Note that the shadowed number 5 represents scale step 5 of the associated C Major Scale*

Therefore, notes G, B, D, and F, when combined as a seventh chord, meet the criteria of a **Dominant Seventh Chord**. That is:

| **Major Third + Minor Third + Minor Third = Dominant Seventh Chord** |
|---|

Moving on, we'll build a seventh chord on Scale Step 6, in this case A. In the example below we see a seventh chord built in intervals of Thirds starting with **A**.

If we analyze the intervals between the notes of this four note seventh chord, we will find the following:

The interval between notes **A** and **C** is a **Minor Third**
The interval between notes **C** and **E** is a **Major Third**
The interval between notes **E** and **G** is a **Minor Third**

*Note that the shadowed number 6 represents scale step 6 of the associated C Major Scale*

Therefore, notes A, C, E, and G, when combined as a seventh chord, meet the criteria of a **Minor Seventh Chord**. That is:

**Minor Third + Major Third + Minor Third = Minor Seventh Chord**

Last, we'll build a seventh chord on Scale Step 7, in this case B. In the final example below we see a seventh chord built in intervals of Thirds starting with **B**.

If we analyze the intervals between the notes of this four note seventh chord, we will find the following:

The interval between notes **B** and **D** is a **Minor Third**
The interval between notes **D** and **F** is a **Minor Third**
The interval between notes **F** and **A** is a **Major Third**

*Note that the shadowed number 7 represents scale step 7 of the associated C Major Scale*

Therefore, notes B, D, F, and A, when combined as a seventh chord, meet the criteria of a **Diminished Seventh Chord**. That is:

**Minor Third + Minor Third + Major Third = Diminished Seventh Chord**

We can now review the pattern that emerges when analyzing the Quality of the Seventh Chords that are built on each step of the Major scale.

- *The 4 note Seventh Chord built on scale step 1 is a* **Major Seventh Chord**
- *The 4 note Seventh Chord built on scale step 2 is a* **Minor Seventh Chord**
- *The 4 note Seventh Chord built on scale step 3 is a* **Minor Seventh Chord**
- *The 4 note Seventh Chord built on scale step 4 is a* **Major Seventh Chord**
- *The 4 note Seventh Chord built on scale step 5 is a* **Dominant Seventh Chord**
- *The 4 note Seventh Chord built on scale step 6 is a* **Minor Seventh Chord**
- *The 4 note Seventh Chord built on scale step 7 is a* **Diminished Seventh Chord**

To simplify: when constructing seventh chords from the numbered notes of a Major scale, the following pattern arises when evaluating the quality of the 4 note chord at each numbered scale step:

> 1 = Major Seventh Chord
> 2 = Minor Seventh Chord
> 3 = Minor Seventh Chord
> 4 = Major Seventh Chord
> 5 = Dominant Seventh Chord
> 6 = Minor Seventh Chord
> 7 = Diminished Seventh Chord

So, in this new emerging pattern:

- *Chords 1 and 4 are qualified as Major Seventh Chords.*
- *Chord 5 is qualified as a Dominant Seventh Chord.*
- *Chords 2, 3, and 6 are qualified as Minor Seventh Chords.*
- *Chord 7 is qualified as a Diminished Seventh Chord.*

Regarding the Dominant Seventh Chord: The Dominant Seventh Chord is utilized in the music of Western societies for its ability to create movement within music. A full explanation of this statement would require a college level music theory class or a lesson on the properties of the Dominant Seventh Chord from a personal music instructor. However, the utility of the Dominant Seventh Chord can be seen in its legendary place in so many recognizable chord progressions. For example, using the chord numbering system, you'll find that when you play chord I (Roman numeral one), followed by chord IV, followed by chord V, your ear will probably want to hear this V chord, the Dominant Seventh Chord, resolve back to chord I. The Roman Numerals used here are: I = 1, IV = 4, and V = 5. The I, IV, V, I chord progression is very recognizable in Blues, Gospel, early Rock & Roll, parts of Classical Music, and pop music. Learning to harness the energy of chord movement (also called chord progression), is at the heart of good musical composition, whether you're composing Rap, Jazz, Folk, Salsa, or Classical Music. Understanding the intricacies of chord progression requires years of study and development. But the basic starting point for almost all serious composers is a solid understanding of Diatonic Harmony. Fully understanding chord progressions can take years of practice and hard work, so be aware that we're only introducing the basics here.

# Chords and Harmony

Since bassists don't need to play chords in the same sense that the pianist and the guitarist play chords, it is important for the bassist to hear chords played harmonically. If you are learning a given piece of music, you may want to ask the pianist or guitarist who you'll be accompanying to write down the names of the chords in the music you'll be playing, and ask them to play (or better yet, record) the chords from the music for you. In this way, you'll have a better understanding of the chord progression and you can use your knowledge of chord construction to create a bassline that will work well with the chord progression. Never underestimate the value of being familiar with the difference in sound of the various chord types - Major, Minor, Dominant, and Diminished. Many bassists miss out on the harmonic dimension of music because they're busy playing bass lines one note at a time (which is how they're supposed to be played). However, since the bass accompanies harmonic instruments, it is very important for the serious bassist to be familiar enough with the sound of the various chord types to be able to distinguish one from another upon hearing them. The more familiar you are with the harmonic dimension of music (specifically, the sound of the various chords), the easier it will be to come up with basslines that are a good fit for the music.

So, if you have access to a piano keyboard, play the various chord types and listen to the sound they make. And if you're learning or creating a bass part for a particular song, have the pianist or guitarist play the chord progression for you on keyboard or guitar, then study not only the notes contained in those chords, but the distinct sound of each type of chord.

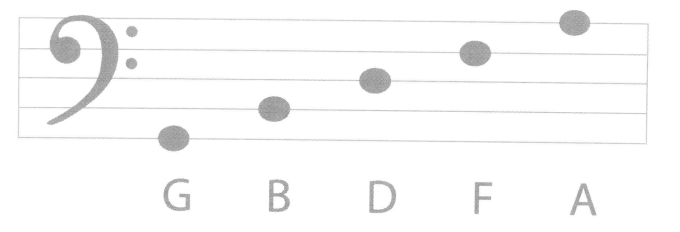

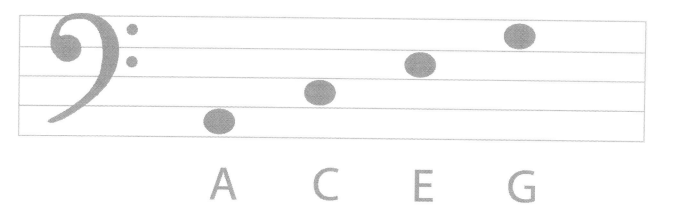

# Chapter 9: Upper Extensions

The "**Upper Extensions**" are the notes/tones that occur if you continue to build a chord in thirds past the seventh of the chord. Chords are constructed in intervals of thirds, so this lesson will discuss the methods used to obtain the Upper Extensions of seventh chords. The chords we've created so far have used only 3 of the available chord tones (triads), or 4 of the available chord tones (seventh chords). There are seven available notes/tones in each of the diatonic modes, and if we rearrange these seven notes so that they're separated by intervals of Thirds, we can utilize all of the available notes when constructing chords, revealing the notes referred to as *upper extensions*.

Because the quality of a chord is basically determined at the triad level, and further defined at the seventh chord level, the upper extensions do not change the quality of a chord. For example, a Major chord which includes the upper extensions of a $9^{th}$, $11^{th}$, and $13^{th}$ is still basically a Major chord, as determined by the relationship of the $3^{rd}$, $5^{th}$, and $7^{th}$ to the Root of the chord. That's good news, because we won't spend a lot of time analyzing chord quality in this lesson.

Let's take a look at what the Upper Extensions are, and where they come from:

We know that there are 7 notes available in a Major Scale.

This illustration shows all the notes of the C Major scale. Because the note at scale step 8 has the same note name as the note in scale step 1, there are seven available note names in the scale.

Since chords are "spelled" (the term sometimes used for constructing chords) in Thirds, a triad uses three of these available notes – the 1 (or root), the 3, and the 5. Similarly, a seventh chord uses four of the notes – the 1, the 3, the 5, and the 7. That leaves out the $2^{nd}$, $4^{th}$, and $6^{th}$ notes of the underling scale (or mode). Chords are built in intervals of Thirds, so if we want to include the notes beyond those already used in the seventh chord, we will need to continue building in thirds beyond the $7^{th}$ of the chord until all seven notes of the underlying scale/mode are accounted for. This is where $2^{nd}$, $4^{th}$, and $6^{th}$ notes are included in the chord as the $9^{th}$, $11^{th}$, and $13^{th}$.

On the next page, we'll look closely at a Major Scale to see what happens to the notes (and their associated numbers) when we rearrange the scale in Thirds (as when we construct chords).

The illustration below shows the notes of the C Major Scale rearranged into Thirds:

This illustration shows all seven notes of the C Major scale rearranged so that each note is separated by an interval distance of a Third.

Constructing a chord in intervals of Thirds requires that you use every other note in the underlying scale or mode. Therefore, in order for all seven scale tones to be included in a chord which is built in Thirds, the chord must span 2 octaves. This span covers 15 notes. This accounts for the use of the terms "9th", "11th", and "13th" for the Upper Extensions of the Seventh Chord.

In the diagram below, the black note names represent all possible notes of the chord. They are an interval of a third apart. The gray notes show all remaining scale steps in numerical order. Note that in order to reach the 9th, 11th and 13th notes, the chord must span two octaves. (See below)

In order for all scale tones to be included in a chord which is built in Thirds, the chord must span 2 octaves. This span covers 15 notes.

This numbering system for chords, which includes the upper extensions, ensures that all available notes are accounted for. In the examples above, we see several things. Specifically:

- Scale Steps 1, 8, and 15 have the same note name - **C**. Scale Step 8 is referred to as the "octave", and scale step 15 as a chord tone is rarely (if ever) referenced in chord construction. 1, 8, and 15 are collectively (and more commonly) referred to as the "Root" of the chord, regardless of which octave they fall in.

- Scale Steps 3, 5, and 7 have the same note names as 10, 12, and 14 respectively, however, when discussing chord tones, it is more common to refer to these chord tones as the third, fifth, and seventh.

- Scale Steps 2, 4, and 6 have the same note names as 9, 11, and 13 respectively, however, when discussing chord tones, it is more common to refer to these chord tones as the ninth, eleventh, and thirteenth.

While the previous examples use the C Major scale and the C Major chord to illustrate the upper extensions, all diatonic chords have upper extensions. The examples below show the upper extensions of the remaining chords in the C Major key center.

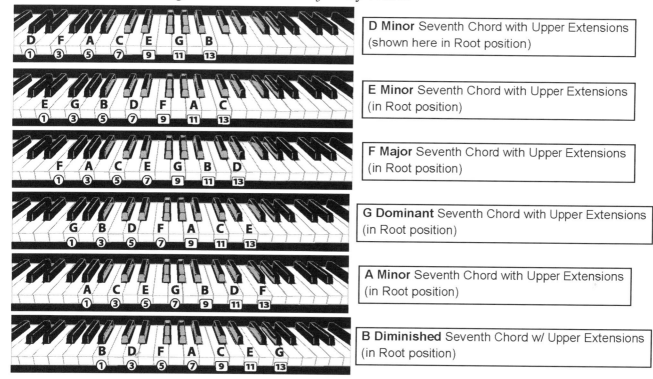

D Minor Seventh Chord with Upper Extensions (shown here in Root position)

E Minor Seventh Chord with Upper Extensions (in Root position)

F Major Seventh Chord with Upper Extensions (in Root position)

G Dominant Seventh Chord with Upper Extensions (in Root position)

A Minor Seventh Chord with Upper Extensions (in Root position)

B Diminished Seventh Chord w/ Upper Extensions (in Root position)

Major chords with upper extensions are referred to as Major 9th, Major 11th, or Major 13th chords. Minor chords with upper extensions are referred to as Minor 9th, Minor 11th, or Minor 13th chords. Dominant chords with upper extensions are simply referred to as 9th, 11th, or 13th chords (because the Dominant chord is often referred to as simply the "Seventh Chord".) Diminished chords are very dissonant when the upper extensions are included, so upper extensions are not commonly used with Diminished chords.

## Chord Voicings

A "chord voicing" is an arrangement of the notes in a chord that may not adhere to rigid construction of creating chords in intervals of thirds with the Root at the bottom. The chord examples in this book are shown in Root position in order to provide a basic understanding of the harmonic structure of chords. Alternatives to root position are sometimes referred to as *inversions*, because while the chord *tones* remain the same (for example 1, 3, 5, 7 or C, E, G, B), an inverted chord may be "voiced" with the 3rd on the bottom, as in 3, 1, 5, 7, or E, C, G, B; still a C Major Seventh chord – just rearranged a bit. While chord voicings and upper extensions are beyond the basics, you should understand their place in the musical palette. Understanding chord voicings can provide any serious musician with a deeper understanding of chord progression and therefore a deeper understanding of music. As a bassist, you should be aware of the upper extensions and their place in Diatonic Harmony.

# Chapter 10:
# Bass Arpeggios using Upper Extensions

The following illustrations will provide you with a way to incorporate upper extensions into your bass playing. These arpeggio examples utilize chord tones 1, 3, 5, 7, 9, and 11. A six note arpeggio is built on each scale step of the key center and includes notes on all four bass strings. There are two separate patterns presented in this chapter: the 1-2-1-2 pattern and the 2-1-2-1 pattern. The 1-2-1-2 pattern starts with 1 note on the E string, followed by 2 notes on the A string, then 1 note again on the D string, ending with 2 notes on the G string. In contrast, the 2-1-2-1 pattern starts with 2 notes on the E string, followed by 1 note on the A string, then 2 notes again on the D string, ending with 1 note on the G string. If this sounds confusing, the illustrations should clear it up.

We'll use arpeggios that only go up to the 11$^{th}$ because on a 4 string bass, you can play these examples without shifting your hand as would be required if we were to incorporate the 13$^{th}$ or the 15$^{th}$ chord tone. Playing the 1-3-5-7-9-11 on each scale step of the Key Center will reveal another group of patterns. These patterns, when played as exercises, are excellent for developing dexterity and fingerboard knowledge.

As a way to establish the patterns that emerge from these arpeggios, we'll again use a symbol as a substitute for note names; this time it's the penny. In the following examples you'll see pennies placed at the points where the note names would normally go. Don't worry about whether you're seeing a new penny or an old one, or whether the penny is on heads or tails. The pennies are just markers.

Here are some things you should be aware of:

Each penny represents a finger placement on the bass fingerboard. As you can see from this illustration, four pennies would represent the placement of each of the four fingers. The strings and frets are represented by the (not so) vertical and horizontal bars. In the interest of clarity, the distance between frets is the same. (On fretted instruments, the distance between frets normally decreases as the notes go higher.)

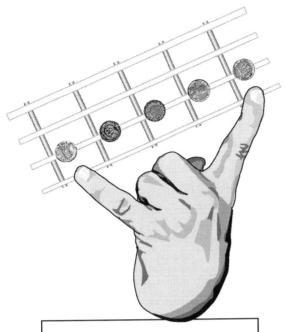

Reaching a distance of 5 Frets can be a stretch.

Many of the arpeggios in the following examples require you to play notes that are 5 frets apart. Since the 5 fret distance is the largest interval in these examples, we'll initially illustrate each arpeggio using five pennies on each of the four strings. This '20 penny' matrix will be our starting point.

Below is an example of the '20 penny' matrix

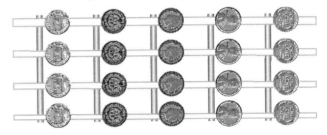

As you review each of the arpeggio examples on the following pages, memorize their shapes and their positions in relation to each other.

Please note that the following examples are provided in the Key of G Major in order to accomodate all of the arpeggios. Please review the Super Scale diagrams shown here in order to become familiar with the G Major Key Center prior to learning the arpeggio patterns.

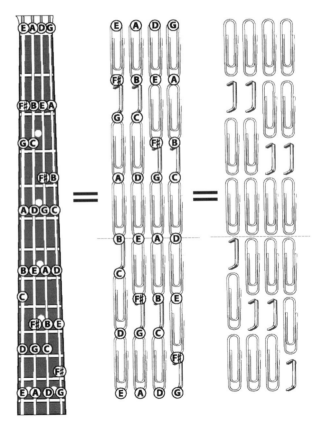

Chapter 10 - Bass Arpeggios

# The 1-2-1-2 Arpeggios

Let's get started with the "1-2-1-2" arpeggios. These arpeggios start with **1** note on the "E" string, followed by **2** notes on the "A" string, then **1** note on the "D" string, ending with **2** notes on the "G" string. While no note names will be displayed, the examples are shown in the key of G Major, since this key will facilitate all seven illustrative examples from the low to the high notes on the bass fingerboard. Once you learn the seven 1-2-1-2 arpeggio patterns, you can apply them in any key and use them as exercises to improve fingerboard knowledge and technique.

## Example 1: the I Major arpeggio

The example below shows the 1-2-1-2 arpeggio that corresponds diatonically to the I (or 'one') Major chord and the Ionian mode.

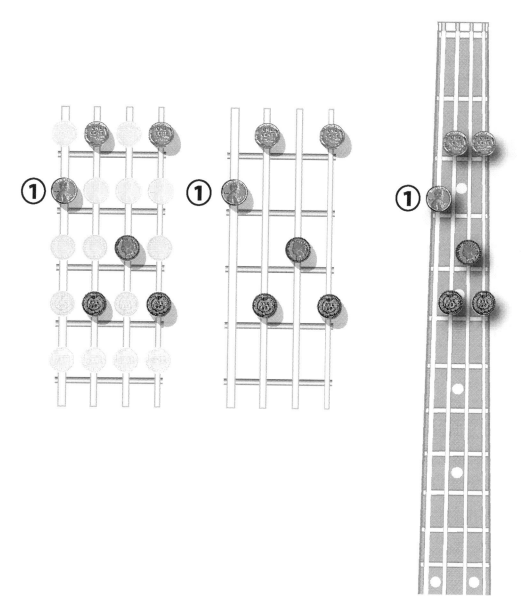

## Example 2: the ii Minor arpeggio

The example below shows the 1-2-1-2 arpeggio that corresponds diatonically to the ii (or 'two') Minor chord and the Dorian mode.

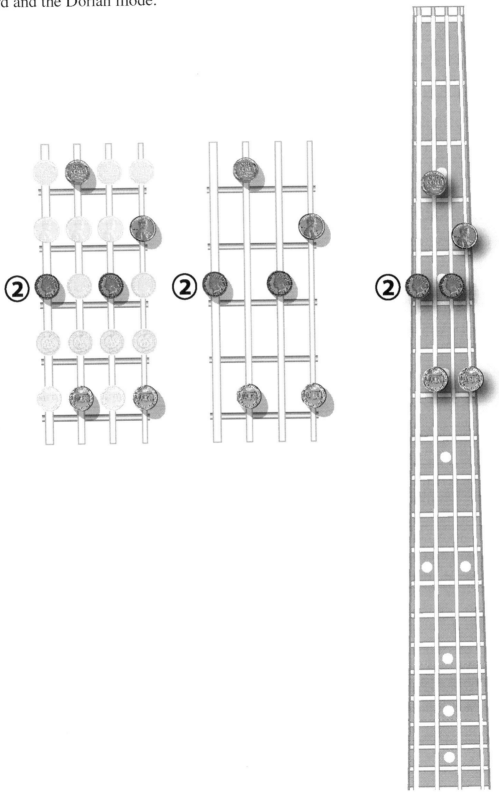

# Example 3: the iii Minor arpeggio

The example below shows the 1-2-1-2 arpeggio that corresponds diatonically to the iii (or 'three') Minor chord and the Phrygian mode.

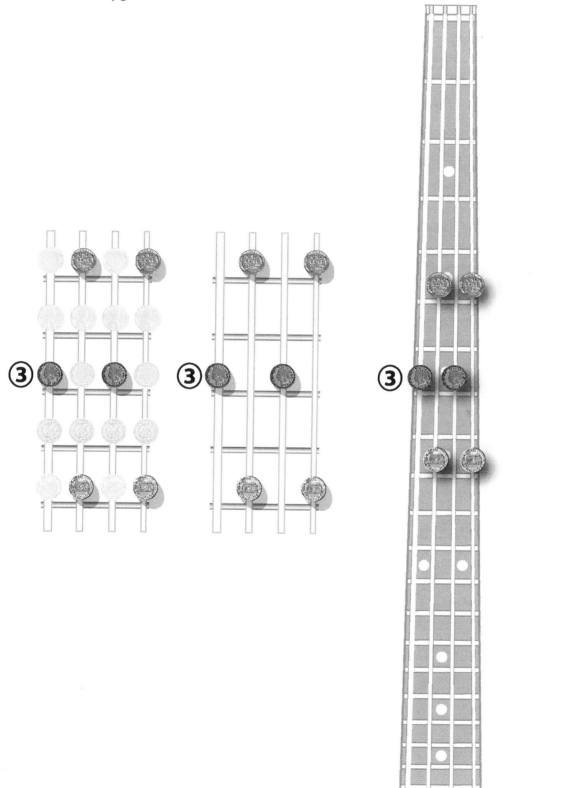

## Example 4: the IV Major arpeggio

The example below shows the 1-2-1-2 arpeggio that corresponds diatonically to the IV (or 'four') Major chord and the Lydian mode.

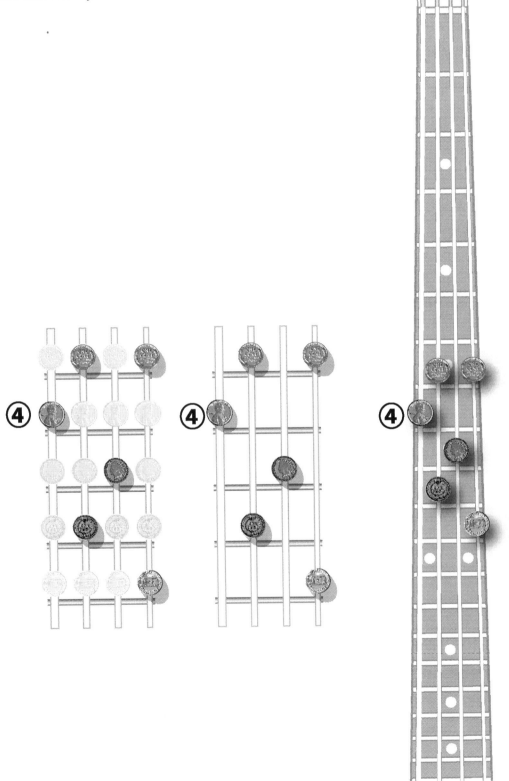

# Example 5: the V Dominant arpeggio

The example below shows the 1-2-1-2 arpeggio that corresponds diatonically to the V (or 'five') Dominant chord and the Mixolydian mode.

Chapter 10 - Bass Arpeggios - The 1-2-1-2 Arpeggios - *the V Dominant arpeggio*

### Example 6: the vi Minor arpeggio

The example below shows the 1-2-1-2 arpeggio that corresponds diatonically to the vi (or 'six') Minor chord and the Aeolian mode.

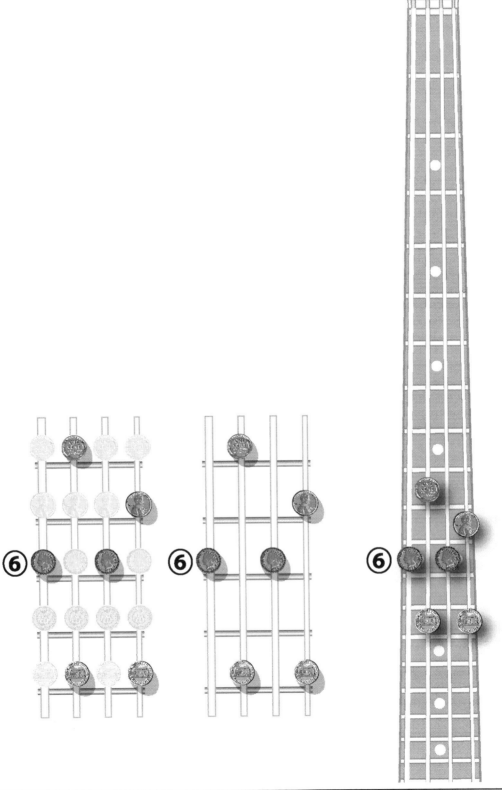

# Example 7: the vii Diminished arpeggio

The example below shows the 1-2-1-2 arpeggio that corresponds diatonically to the vii (or 'seven') Diminished chord and the Locrian mode.

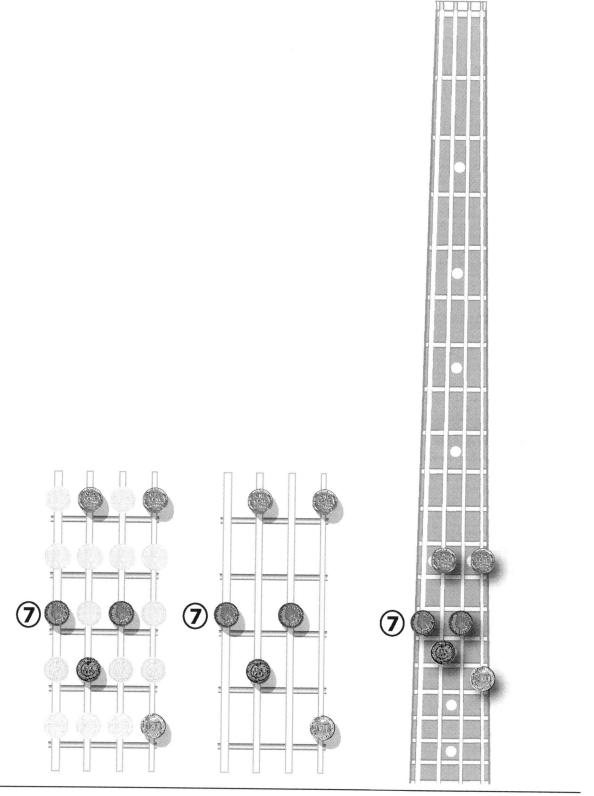

Below is a chart showing all of the 1-2-1-2 arpeggio shapes:

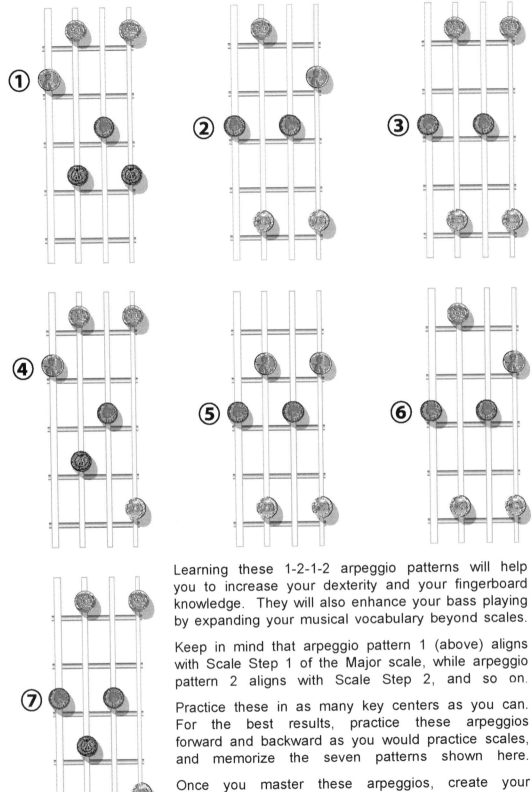

Learning these 1-2-1-2 arpeggio patterns will help you to increase your dexterity and your fingerboard knowledge. They will also enhance your bass playing by expanding your musical vocabulary beyond scales.

Keep in mind that arpeggio pattern 1 (above) aligns with Scale Step 1 of the Major scale, while arpeggio pattern 2 aligns with Scale Step 2, and so on.

Practice these in as many key centers as you can. For the best results, practice these arpeggios forward and backward as you would practice scales, and memorize the seven patterns shown here.

Once you master these arpeggios, create your own arpeggio patterns. Also, be aware that these patterns align with the Super Scale pattern.

# The 2-1-2-1 Arpeggios

Now we'll look at the "2-1-2-1" arpeggios. These arpeggios start with 2 notes on the "E" string, followed by 1 note on the "A" string, then 2 notes on the "D" string, ending with 1 note on the "G" string. While no note names will be displayed, the examples are shown in the key of G Major, since this key will facilitate all seven illustrative examples from the low to the high notes on the bass fingerboard. Once you learn the seven 2-1-2-1 arpeggio patterns, you can apply them in any key and use them as exercises to improve fingerboard knowledge and technique.

## Example 1: the I Major arpeggio

The example below shows the 2-1-2-1 arpeggio that corresponds diatonically to the I (or 'one') Major chord and the Ionian mode.

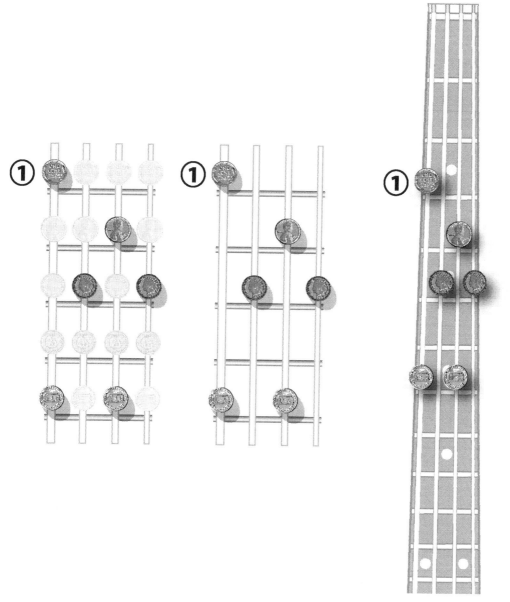

## Example 2: the ii Minor arpeggio

The example below shows the 2-1-2-1 arpeggio that corresponds diatonically to the ii (or 'two') Minor chord and the Dorian mode.

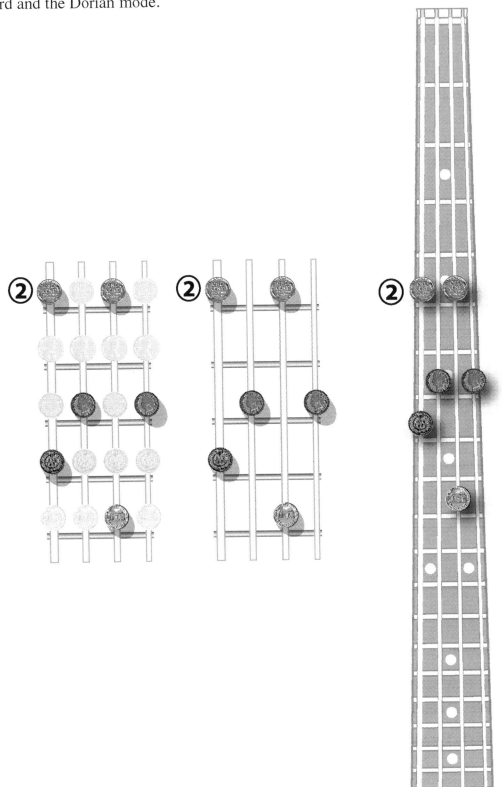

# Example 3: the iii Minor arpeggio

The example below shows the 2-1-2-1 arpeggio that corresponds diatonically to the iii (or 'three') Minor chord and the Phrygian mode.

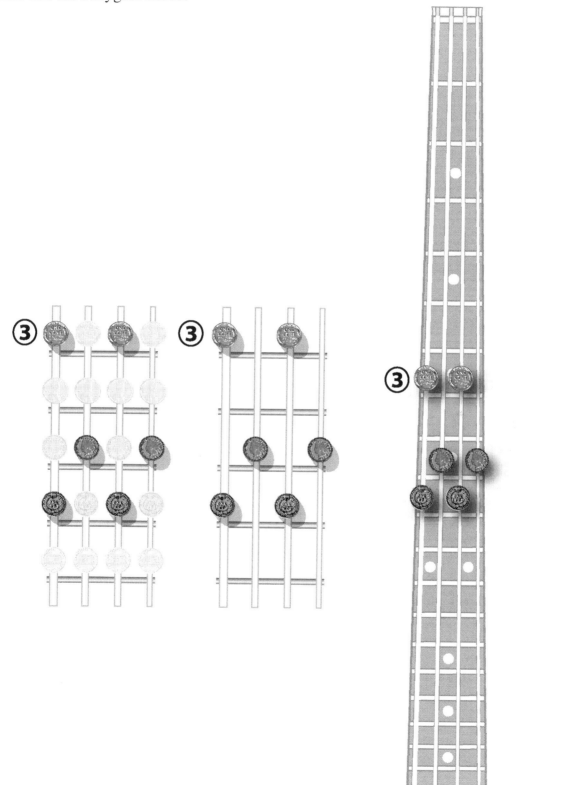

## Example 4: the IV Major arpeggio

The example below shows the 2-1-2-1 arpeggio that corresponds diatonically to the IV (or 'four') Major chord and the Lydian mode.

Chapter 10 - Bass Arpeggios - The 2-1-2-1 Arpeggios - *the IV Major arpeggio*

# Example 5: the V Dominant arpeggio

The example below shows the 2-1-2-1 arpeggio that corresponds diatonically to the V (or 'five') Dominant chord and the Mixolydian mode.

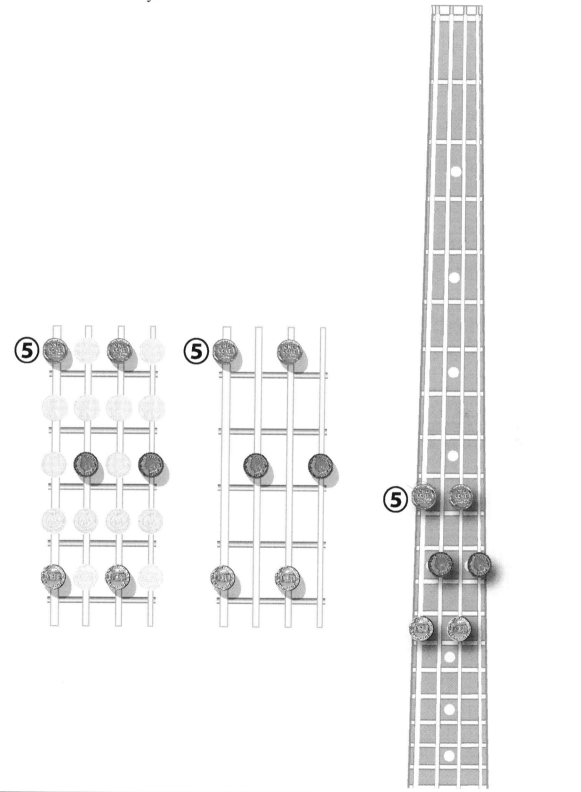

# Example 6: the vi Minor arpeggio

The example below shows the 2-1-2-1 arpeggio that corresponds diatonically to the vi (or 'six') Minor chord and the Aeolian mode.

# Example 7: the vii Diminished arpeggio

The example below shows the 2-1-2-1 arpeggio that corresponds diatonically to the vii (or 'seven') Diminished chord and the Locrian mode.

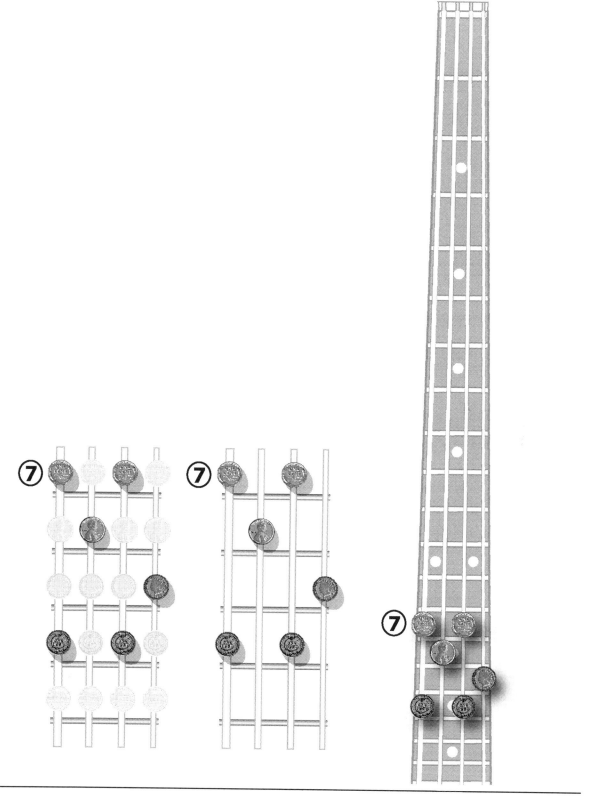

Below is a chart showing all of the 2-1-2-1 arpeggio shapes:

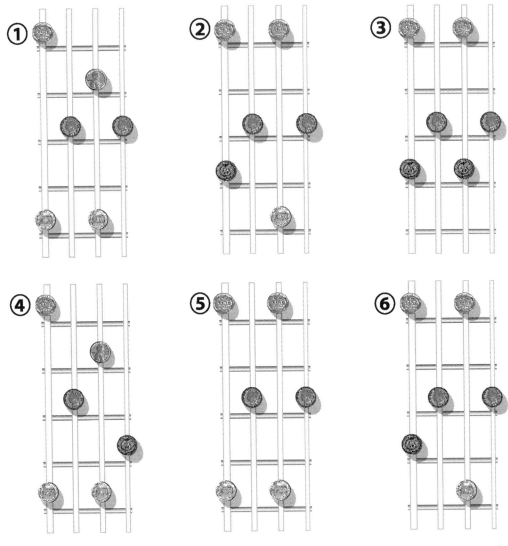

Learning these 2-1-2-1 arpeggio patterns will help you to increase your dexterity and your fingerboard knowledge. They will also enhance your bass playing by expanding your musical vocabulary beyond scales.

Keep in mind that arpeggio pattern 1 (above) aligns with Scale Step 1 of the Major scale, while arpeggio pattern 2 aligns with Scale Step 2, and so on.

Practice these in as many key centers as you can. For the best results, practice these arpeggios forward and backward as you would practice scales, and memorize the seven patterns shown here.

Once you master these arpeggios, create your own arpeggio patterns. Also, be aware that these patterns align with the Super Scale pattern.

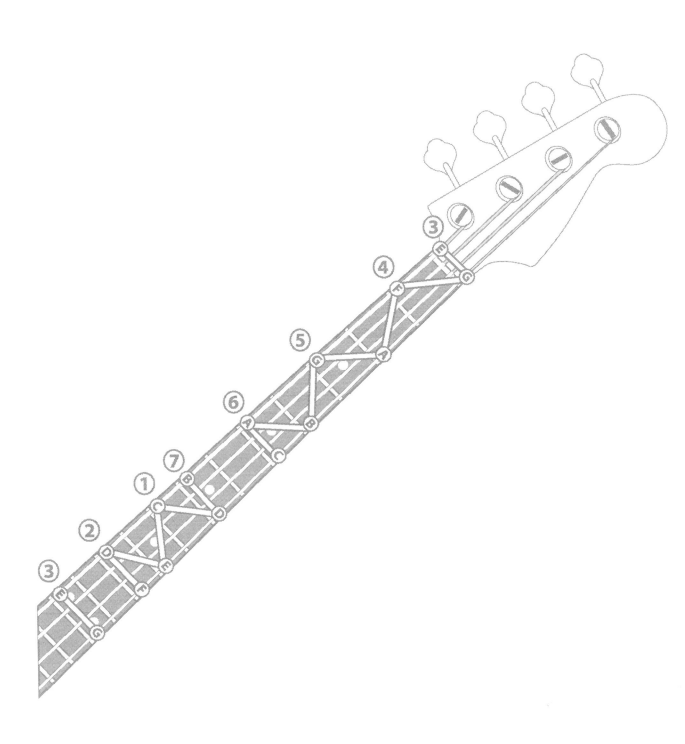

# Chapter 11: The Other Intervals

So far, we've learned about the Intervals called **Seconds** and **Thirds**. Now let's learn about the remaining intervals. Below is a list of all the intervals and an explanation of the number of whole steps and half steps contained within each:

| Interval Name | Distance between notes |
|---|---|
| Unison | same note |
| Minor Second | 1 half step, 2 note names |
| Major Second | 1 whole step, 2 note names |
| Minor Third | 1 whole step + 1 half step, 3 note names |
| Major Third | 2 whole steps, 3 note names |
| Perfect Fourth | 2 whole steps + 1 half step, 4 note names |
| Tritone | 3 whole steps, 4 or 5 note names (example – from C to F♯ or from C to G♭) |
| Perfect Fifth | 3 whole steps + 1 half step, 5 note names |
| Minor Sixth | 4 whole steps, 6 note names |
| Major Sixth | 4 whole steps + 1 half step, 6 note names |
| Minor Seventh | 5 whole steps, 7 note names |
| Major Seventh | 5 whole steps + 1 half step, 7 note names |
| Octave | 6 whole steps, 8 note names |

As is the case with most of music theory, things come to life when you hear them in action. This is very true when it comes to intervals. Knowledge of intervals can help you to create more interesting, less "scale-like" melodies and basslines. Experts in improvisation employ intervals in their playing as a way to add variety and interest to their solos. Let's take a look at the intervals as they appear on the bass fingerboard. Since the Unison is the same note, and we've covered Seconds and Thirds, we'll start with the interval of a Perfect Fourth.

## The Perfect Fourth:

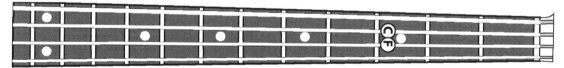

The illustration above shows the shape of a Perfect Fourth interval on the bass fingerboard.

## The Tritone:

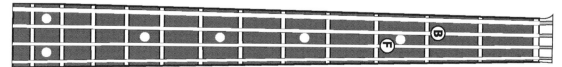

The illustration above shows the shape of a Tritone interval on the bass fingerboard.

### The Perfect Fifth - option 1:

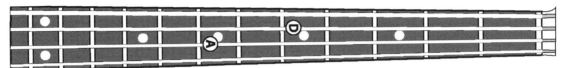

The illustration above shows the shape of a Perfect Fifth interval on the bass fingerboard.

### The Perfect Fifth - option 2:

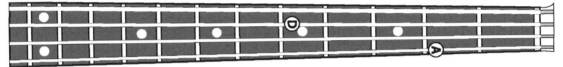

The illustration above also shows the shape of a Perfect Fifth interval on the bass fingerboard.

### The Minor Sixth - option 1:

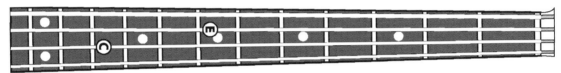

The illustration above shows the shape of a Minor Sixth interval on the bass fingerboard.

### The Minor Sixth - option 2:

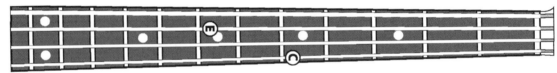

The illustration above also shows the shape of a Minor Sixth interval on the bass fingerboard.

### The Major Sixth - option 1:

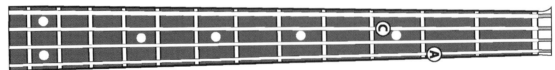

The illustration above shows the shape of a Major Sixth interval on the bass fingerboard.

### The Major Sixth - option 2:

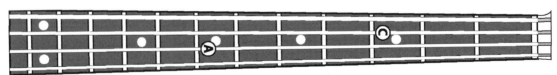

The illustration above also shows the shape of a Major Sixth interval on the bass fingerboard.

## The Minor Seventh:

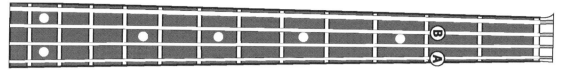

The illustration above shows the shape of a Minor Seventh interval on the bass fingerboard.

## The Major Seventh:

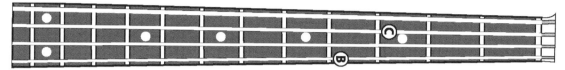

The illustration above shows the shape of a Major Seventh interval on the bass fingerboard.

## The Octave - option 1:

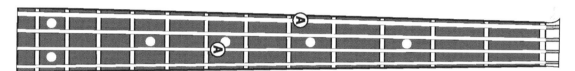

The illustration above shows the shape of an Octave interval on the bass fingerboard.

## The Octave - option 2:

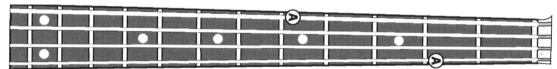

The illustration above also shows the shape of an Octave interval on the bass fingerboard.

# Beyond the Octave

As you might have guessed, there are upper intervals from the Minor 9th to the Major 13th, but these are generally the territory of a more advanced study of music. However, here are a few of the intervals beyond an octave that are very useful to the bassist.

*Note: Because the Minor Ninth is very dissonant, and therefore doesn't sound very good on a bass, we'll skip it and start with the Major Ninth, which sounds great on the bass*

## The Major Ninth:

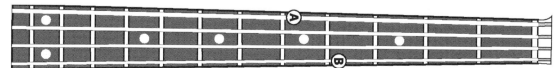

The illustration above shows the shape of a Major Ninth interval on the bass fingerboard.

### The Minor Tenth:

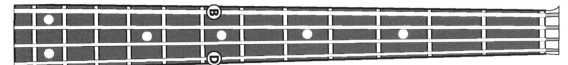

The illustration above shows the shape of a Minor Tenth interval on the bass fingerboard.

### The Major Tenth:

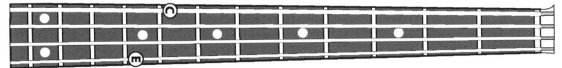

The illustration above shows the shape of a Major Tenth interval on the bass fingerboard.

### The Eleventh:

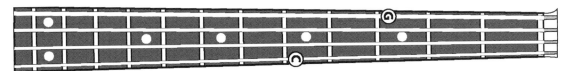

The illustration above shows the shape of an Eleventh interval on the bass fingerboard.

By learning these intervals and incorporating them into your playing, you can add melodic interest to the basslines you create. Musicians who only practice using scales tend to sound very scaly (like lizards or fish) when they play. Don't be a lizard. Incorporate intervals into your practice routine.

Another way to bring the intervals to life while you're learning them is to associate the various intervals with recognizable parts of popular songs, jingles, and melodies. By identifying intervals contained in these melodies, you can learn to recognize the individual intervals when you hear them. While this may sound like a waste of time, the ability to recognize intervals upon hearing them is useful for learning music "by ear" if you don't have a written transcript of that music. Whether you are trying to learn or transcribe a bass line, a guitar solo, a horn solo, or a vocal melody, knowledge of intervals will make this task easier. One example of a popular melody that contains a Major Second is the "Happy Birthday" song (which is sung at kids' birthday parties). There are web sites devoted to listing tunes that embody the intervals. Take some time to play these intervals and listen to them to hear if there are any similarities between the interval and any songs, jingles, or melodies that you know. If so, make a list of all of the intervals and try to identify any songs, jingles, or melodies that contain these intervals.

Experienced bassists use intervals to contour their bass solos. By starting a solo with smaller intervals such as seconds and thirds, then expanding to include fourths, fifths, and sixths, all the way up to thirteenths, they increase the melodic complexity as they develop their solo. An experienced bassist might start a bass solo with notes that are somewhat scale-like, and end a solo playing notes that are arpeggiated. While this type of playing can take years to master, it starts with the knowledge of intervals.

# More information on Ninths and Tenths

The diagrams below show the pattern of ninths and tenths as they exist in the key of C Major.

The numbers next to the fret board below represent the scale steps of the C Major scale. The lines between the dots reveal the pattern of Major Ninths, Minor Tenths, and Major Tenths. These intervals, when played melodically or harmonically, will provide you with a way to expand your musical vocabulary while utilizing the outer interval combinations on the fingerboard of the 4 string bass.

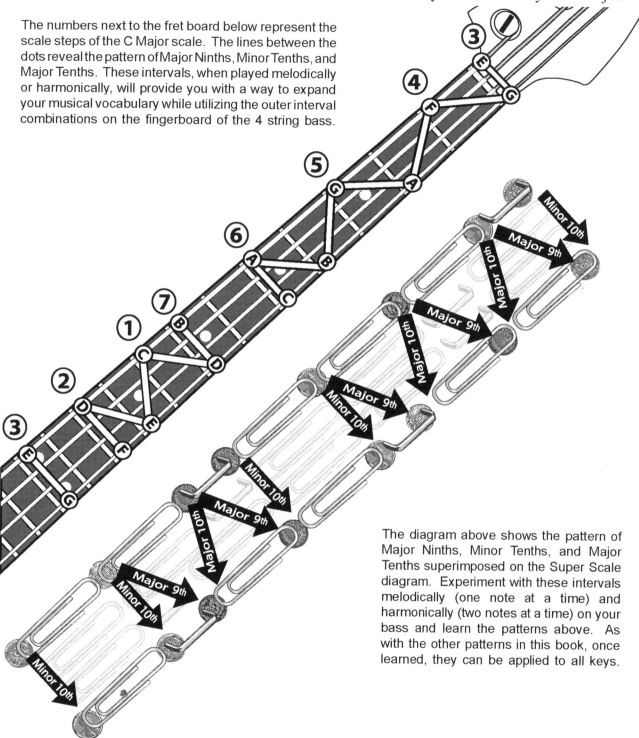

The diagram above shows the pattern of Major Ninths, Minor Tenths, and Major Tenths superimposed on the Super Scale diagram. Experiment with these intervals melodically (one note at a time) and harmonically (two notes at a time) on your bass and learn the patterns above. As with the other patterns in this book, once learned, they can be applied to all keys.

Again, include intervals in addition to scales and arpeggios when you practice.

# Chapter 12: Mode and Chord Relationships

Now that we've reviewed the Diatonic Harmony scheme, which reveals the pattern of chord quality for chords built upon the seven scale steps, let's take a closer look at the modes. Because modes are scales built upon each step of the Major Scale, they will share similar properties to chords. Recall that in the Diatonic Harmony scheme, seventh chords follow this pattern:

```
1 = Major Seventh Chord
2 = Minor Seventh Chord
3 = Minor Seventh Chord
4 = Major Seventh Chord
5 = Dominant Seventh Chord
6 = Minor Seventh Chord
7 = Diminished Seventh Chord
```

The seven modes are built upon the same scale steps that the seven diatonic chords (above) are built upon. Because of this, each mode matches up with a related chord. This brings us to the next topic – using modes and chords together.

As you may have guessed by now, since the Modes match the quality of the Chords in Diatonic Harmony, the modes often go hand in hand with the chords when creating melodies. An understanding of this relationship between the modes and the diatonic chords is as critical to serious composers as it is to improvising musicians who play jazz, blues, or rock. The table below shows the Diatonic Chords and their associated modes.

| Scale Step | Seventh Chord type | Mode name |
|---|---|---|
| 1 or I | Major | Ionian (major scale) |
| 2 or ii | Minor | Dorian |
| 3 or iii | Minor | Phrygian |
| 4 or IV | Major | Lydian |
| 5 or V | Dominant | Mixolydian |
| 6 or vi | Minor | Aeolian (natural minor) |
| 7 or vii° | Diminished | Locrian |

To further explore the relationship between the chords and the modes, let's look at the **ii, V, I** (two, five, one) chord progression.

The chart above shows that the **ii** (two) chord is a minor chord and the associated mode is the Dorian mode. Therefore, if you know that you are playing through a **ii, V, I** chord progression, you can play the Dorian mode to create the bassline to accompany the **ii** chord.

In the same way, looking at the chart shows that the **V** (*five*) chord is a Dominant chord and the associated mode is the Mixolydian mode. Therefore, when playing through a **ii,V,I** chord progression, you can play the Mixolydian mode to create the bassline that accompanies the **V** chord.

Similarly, looking at the chart shows that the **I** (*one*) chord is a major chord and the associated mode is the Ionian mode, which is a major scale. Theoretically, when playing through a **ii,V,I** chord progression, you could play the Ionian mode to create the bassline to accompany the **I** chord. However, the **I** (*one*) chord may sometimes be something other than a Major chord. In that case, you would need to evaluate the best mode for the job. In cases like this, you can refer to the chart on the previous page for help in deciding which mode will best match the chord.

## Progressions and Key Centers

Music theory is the advanced study of music. Often times, the student of music theory is asked to take a piece of written music with no chord symbol markings and determine by looking at the notes in that written music, the key center and underlying chords and chord progressions of that music. The knowledge required to evaluate key centers and chord progressions can also be very useful for the improvising musician or songwriter. In the case of the improvising musician, this knowledge can be very useful in determining the key center of a given chord progression. Knowing the key center of the music being played can provide the improvising musician with more freedom to play.

For example, let's take the situation of a bassist creating a bassline for a **iii, vi, ii, V, I** (*three, six, two, five, one*) chord progression. If you look at the chart on the previous page, you can see that the **iii** (*three*) chord is associated with the third scale step, the **vi** (*six*) chord is associated with the sixth scale step, the **ii** (*two*) chord is associated with the second scale step, the **V** (*five*) with the fifth scale step, and the **I** (*one*) with the first scale step (which is the key center if the music is in a Major rather than a minor key). If the song is moving quickly, it can be very difficult for the musician to formulate an improvisational plan if he's calculating that the **iii** chord gets a Phrygian mode, the **vi** chord gets an Aeolian mode, the **ii** chord gets a Dorian mode, the **V** chord gets a Mixolydian mode, and the **I** chord gets a Ionian (or other) mode. However, if the improvising musician takes the time in advance to evaluate the chord progression and determine the key center, he might realize that he only needs to play notes which are in the key center during this **iii, vi, ii, V, I** passage. That is where the ability to determine key centers from chord progressions can go hand in hand with the pattern referred to earlier as the "Super Scale". Once you determine the key center, you can align the Super Scale properly and play all of the correct chord tones.

Of course, there's more to life than just correct chord tones. In the next chapter, you'll learn about the Pentatonic Scale. While an experienced bassist might use modes to create a bassline to accompany the iii, vi, ii, V, I (*three, six, two, five, one*) chord progression described above, they might use a Pentatonic Scale with a Flat 5th (known as a "Blues Scale") to solo over a song that contains this chord progression. While Diatonic notes are a safe bet when creating basslines, experienced bassists prefer more choices. There are blues notes, passing tones (or passing notes), whole tone scales, harmonic and melodic minor scales. Nonetheless, a solid grasp of Diatonic Harmony will go a long way toward allowing you to play more freely in improvisational situations.

Determining the Tonality, or Key Center, of whatever you're playing requires knowledge of both diatonic harmony, chord construction, key signatures, and scales (in many keys) to fully understand. This is especially true if the music modulates to a different key center. It can take years of practice to become proficient at musical improvisation.

There are many commonly used Chord Progressions repeated throughout Western music. (Western as opposed to Eastern music which employs the quarter tone system). There's the Blues Progression based on the **I, IV, V** (one, four, five), the jazz **ii, V, I** (two, five, one) Chord Progression (referred to by jazzers as a "two-five-one turnaround"). There's the more complex **iii, vi, ii, V, I** (3, 6, 2, 5, 1) turnaround that would also be familiar to jazz musicians. There are Modal chord progressions, Minor chord progressions, and chord progressions that modulate from one key center to another. Much more than can be covered by this basic book.

The study of music is a life long commitment. Musicians can get better at their chosen instrument as they get older. If you gain a firm grasp of the basics of diatonic harmony as it relates to chords, modes, and other scales, you will be much less likely to become bored with your instrument because you'll have a solid base from which you can continue to explore music.

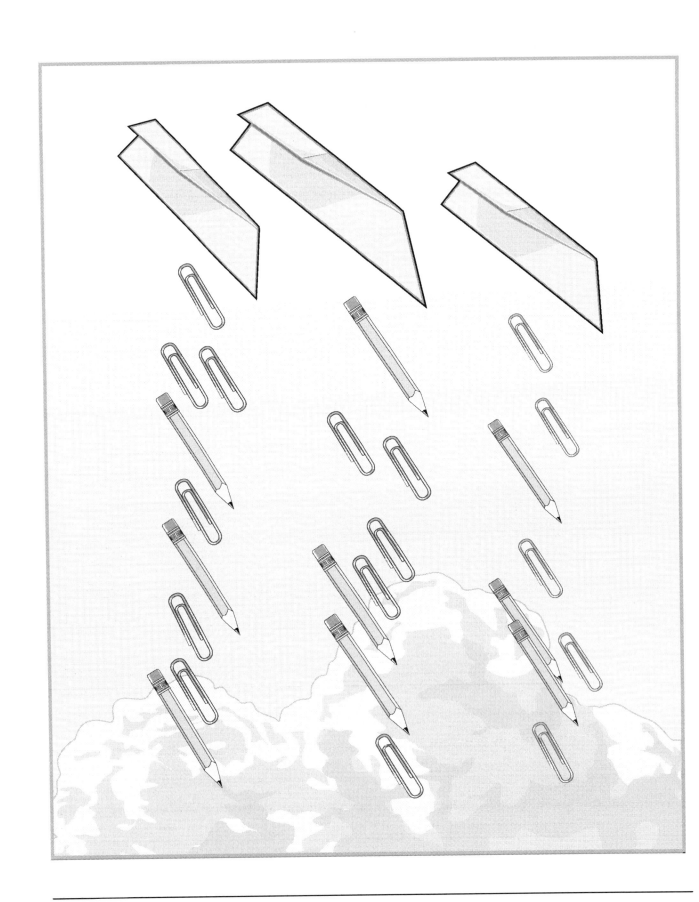

Chapter 13 - The Pentatonic Scale

# Chapter 13: The Pentatonic Scale

Up to this point, you have been learning scales that strictly use only Diatonic notes. One of the most prominent non-diatonic scales is the Pentatonic Scale.

## The Pentatonic Scale

The Pentatonic Scale is a 5 note scale that seems simple enough, yet is loaded with potential. This pentatonic scale is highly regarded by jazz, blues, and rock musicians worldwide, and it is critical that you, as a bassist, learn this scale. Because it's a 5 note scale, it can be substituted for the modes, so it can liberate you from playing that sounds scale-like. The Pentatonic Scale is a hybrid scale. There are 2 types of pentatonic scale: the Major Pentatonic, and the Minor Pentatonic. The Minor Pentatonic scale includes only the root, third, fourth, fifth, and seventh notes of any given "minor type" mode. The Major Pentatonic scale includes only the root, second, third, fifth, and sixth notes of any given "major type" mode.

As a starting point, let's take a look at the Major and Minor Pentatonic scales in root position.

### The Major Pentatonic Scale

The illustration below shows the basic pattern of a Major Pentatonic Scale in root position.

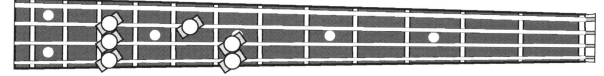

### The Minor Pentatonic Scale

The illustration below shows the basic pattern of a Minor Pentatonic Scale in root position.

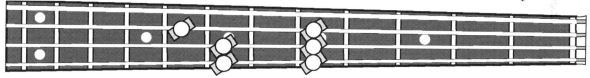

### Pentatonic Scale: the Ultimate Substitute

The pentatonic scale is an amazing substitute for the modes because the Major Pentatonic scale shares 5 notes in common with each of the three Major type modes and the Minor Pentatonic scale shares 5 notes in common with each of the three Minor type modes. In order to see the common notes, pentatonic scales have been superimposed over the modes in the illustrations that follow. We'll take a look at Major and Minor separately. In the following illustrations, you might notice that the notes which do not coincide with the pentatonic scale tones (the notes represented by a white letter inside a black circle) are also the notes that distinguish the modes and give each mode its own "personality". Because the Pentatonic scales (Major and Minor) do not include these distinguishing notes, Pentatonic scales make excellent substitutes for modes. The only rule would be that the Major Pentatonic scale be substituted for a Major type mode, and a Minor Pentatonic scale be substituted for a Minor type mode.

*Before we start, here's a key to the diagrams:*

| Icon | Purpose |
|---|---|
| ◇ | Pentatonic scale note |
| Ⓕ | Modal scale note which also occurs in the Pentatonic scale |
| Ⓔ | Modal scale note which does not occur in the Pentatonic scale |
| ⊗ | Pentatonic scale note with no matching Modal scale note |

## Comparing the Major Pentatonic Scale to the Major type modes:

Let's take a look at the Major Pentatonic scale superimposed over the Ionian Mode (the Major Scale):

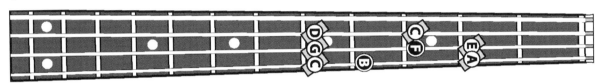

As you can see from the above illustration, the Major Pentatonic scale shares 5 notes in common with the Ionian mode, or Major scale.

Now let's look at the Major Pentatonic scale superimposed over the Lydian Mode:

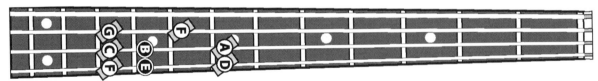

The above illustration shows that the Major Pentatonic scale shares 5 notes in common with the Lydian mode.

Finally we'll look at the Major Pentatonic scale superimposed over the Mixolydian Mode:

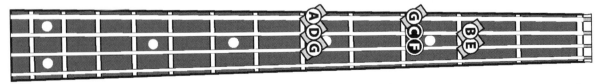

The illustration above shows that the Major Pentatonic scale shares 5 notes in common with the Mixolydian mode.

## Comparing the Minor Pentatonic Scale to the Minor type modes:

Let's switch to the Minor Pentatonic scale now. We'll start by looking at the Minor Pentatonic scale superimposed over the Dorian Mode:

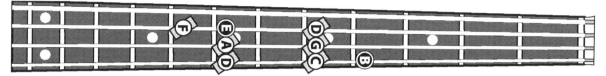

As you can see from the above illustration, the Minor Pentatonic scale shares 5 notes in common with the Dorian mode.

Now let's look at the Minor Pentatonic scale superimposed over the Phrygian Mode:

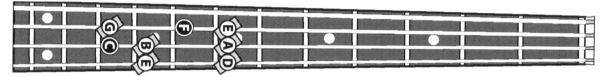

The above illustration shows that the Minor Pentatonic scale shares 5 notes in common with the Phrygian mode.

Let's take a look at the Minor Pentatonic scale superimposed over the Aeolian Mode (the Natural Minor Scale):

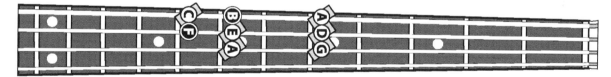

The above illustration shows that the Minor Pentatonic scale shares 5 notes in common with the Aeolian mode, or Natural Minor Scale.

Again, notice that in the previous examples, the notes which do not coincide with the pentatonic scale tones (the notes represented by a white letter inside a black circle) are the notes that give each mode its own "personality". Because the Pentatonic scales (Major and Minor) do not include these distinguishing notes, Pentatonic scales make excellent substitutes for modes. Just remember that a Major Pentatonic scale can be substituted for any Major type mode, and a Minor Pentatonic scale can be substituted for any Minor type mode. Substituting the Pentatonic scale for the modes can be especially useful when improvising on the spot on a tune you might not be familiar with.

### Accept no substitutes: The Locrian Mode

Last, we'll look at the Minor Pentatonic scale superimposed over the Locrian Mode:

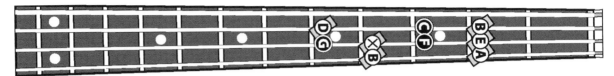

As you can see from the above illustration, the Minor Pentatonic scale has only 4 notes in common with the Locrian mode. The Locrian mode is actually a Diminished scale. Because of this, the Minor Pentatonic is not a good substitute for the Locrian mode.

## The Pentatonic "Super Scale" Pattern

Because of the importance of the Pentatonic Scale, we'll learn the Pentatonic Scale on four strings, then on two strings, then on one string. This may seem like a strange way to learn a scale, but it will help you to see the scale in a wider perspective than just "root position". Learning the pentatonic scale on 4 strings will reveal the "Pentatonic Super Scale" pattern, which encompasses the whole fingerboard and, as you will see, shares similar features to the Diatonic Super Scale.

The pentatonic scale contains only Major Second (whole step) and Minor Third intervals. For the purpose of simplification and visualization, we're going to convert Major Seconds and Minor Thirds to symbols in order to enable us to see the patterns within the scale. Keeping in mind that a Minor Third is equal to one Major Second plus a Minor Second (a whole step plus a half step), we'll use a household item to help us visualize this. We'll continue to use the paper clip as a substitute for a Major Second. But in order to make it easier to visualize the interval of a Minor Third, we'll substitute a pencil for this interval.

Let's take a look at the pencil as a substitute for the Minor Third interval:

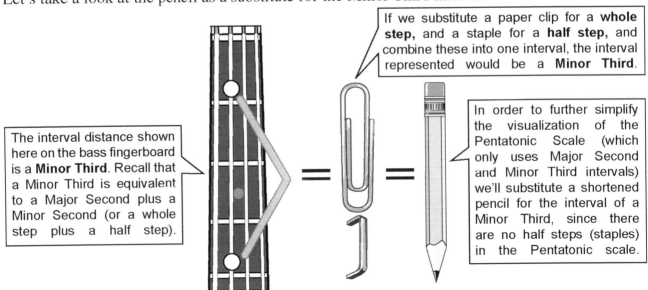

If we substitute a paper clip for a **whole step**, and a staple for a **half step**, and combine these into one interval, the interval represented would be a **Minor Third**.

The interval distance shown here on the bass fingerboard is a **Minor Third**. Recall that a Minor Third is equivalent to a Major Second plus a Minor Second (or a whole step plus a half step).

In order to further simplify the visualization of the Pentatonic Scale (which only uses Major Second and Minor Third intervals) we'll substitute a shortened pencil for the interval of a Minor Third, since there are no half steps (staples) in the Pentatonic scale.

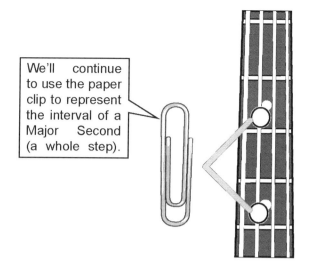

We'll continue to use the paper clip to represent the interval of a Major Second (a whole step).

Understand that there is no official musical reason to substitute pencils, staples, and paper clips for intervals. The only purpose here is to create a visual map of the Pentatonic Scale on the bass fingerboard in order to make the underlying patterns more apparent, and hopefully therefore, easier to memorize. By memorizing the scale patterns, you can more easily apply the scale in any key while playing.

## The Pentatonic Super Scale

This illustration compares the E Minor Pentatonic scale as shown on the bass fingerboard to the pattern map of the Pentatonic Scale in order to see the patterns that emerge:

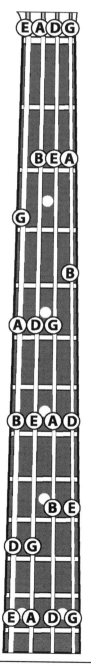
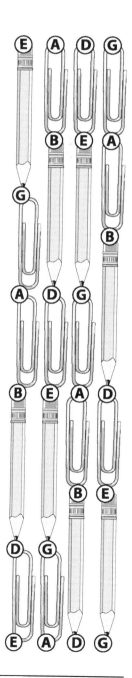

Let's take a closer look at this Pentatonic Super Scale pattern and break the master pattern down for the purpose of further simplifying the task of memorizing it. By memorizing this pattern, you will be able to see the pattern in your mind (overlaid on your fingerboard) which will allow you to access every note in the scale on every string as you play, up and down the bass fingerboard. This should help you to utilize your four- string bass to its fullest potential.

## Analyzing the Pentatonic Super Scale

As mentioned previously, the Pentatonic Scale has two distinct parts. Separating the pattern into two parts allows you to see specific features of each part. This should make the whole pattern easier to memorize. The illustration below identifies these 2 parts of the master pattern. If you look at the separate halves, you might notice that each half contains a separate pattern, and just as we saw with the Diatonic pattern, even if you spin each of the halves upside down (by rotating them), they retain the same Minor Third and Major Second pattern. By breaking down the pattern and learning each half separately, you can more easily learn the entire pattern. Learning both halves of the pattern will go a long way toward mastery of the Pentatonic Scale in any key on the bass fingerboard.

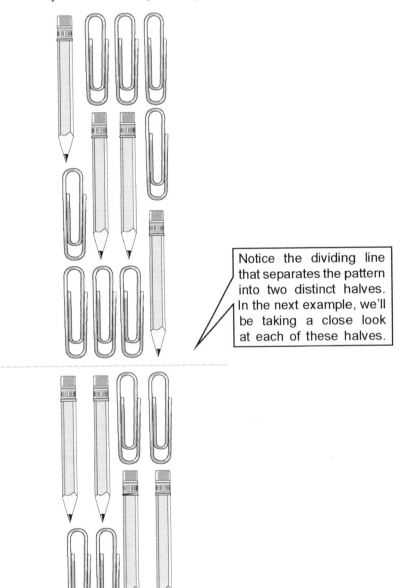

Notice the dividing line that separates the pattern into two distinct halves. In the next example, we'll be taking a close look at each of these halves.

Let's look at the top half of the pattern shown on the previous page. You'll notice that the Minor Third and Major Second patterns are identical, even when this pattern is flipped upside-down by rotating clockwise:

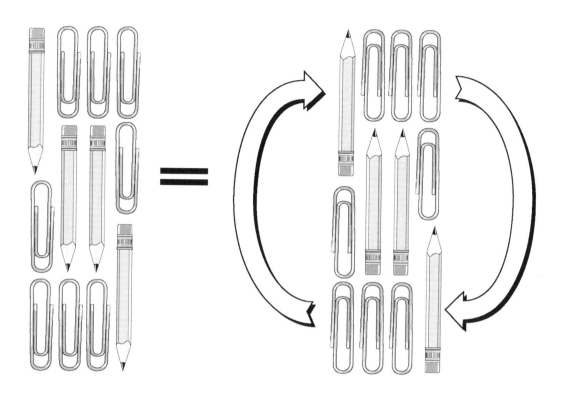

The same holds true for the lower half of the pattern shown on the previous page:

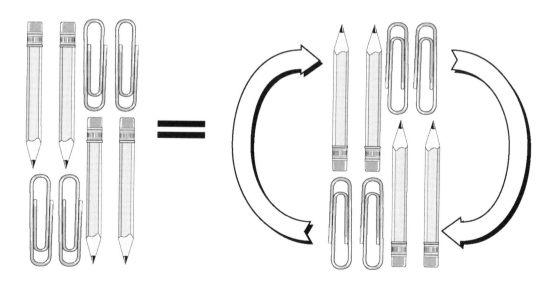

Next, we'll look at the way these two patterns alternate. Be aware that depending on what you are playing, the pattern that has been pictured on top might actually be the lower half of the pattern and vice-versa.

Chapter 13 - The Pentatonic Scale - Analyzing the Pentatonic Super Scale

The illustration below shows how the two halves of the pattern alternate (regardless of which half is on top):

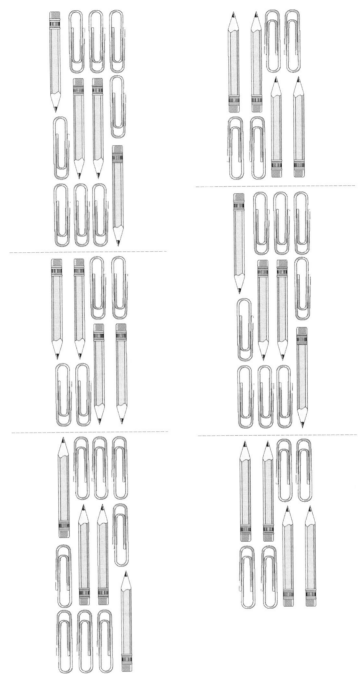

Again, the goal in removing all of the note names, etc., is to simplify the process of learning the pentatonic scales in any key on your fingerboard. It is quite common in the study of music theory to seek patterns that can be applied across any key. Hopefully, this Pentatonic Super Scale will enable you to see the Pentatonic Scale on the bass fingerboard more clearly and completely.

In addition to enabling you to visualize the master pattern across all four strings of the bass, it is possible to use the pencil/paper clip comparison to see the patterns that emerge on one and then two strings. Take a look at the following examples and play the one string and two string patterns on your bass. Playing all of these patterns (1, 2, and 4 string) will help you to commit them to memory. We'll start with the one string pattern:

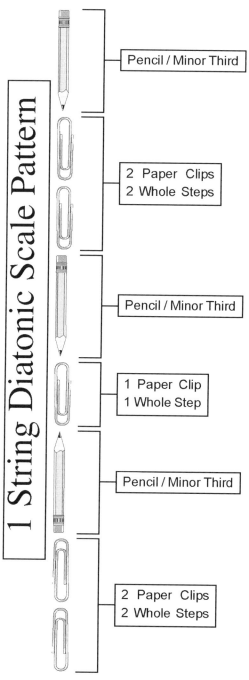

As you can see, the basic pentatonic pattern on one string is: Minor Third, two Major Seconds, Minor Third, one Major Second, Minor Third, two Major Seconds. This one string pattern repeats, and it applies to both Major and Minor Pentatonic scales.

At this point, we'll introduce one more substitution icon which we'll utilize twice in the 2 string pentatonic pattern: the paper airplane. The paper airplane as used here represents the first four notes of each type of pentatonic scale - Major and Minor. The following illustrations will show that the first four notes of either type scale are arranged in such a way that if you were to draw a line from note-dot to note-dot, the shape would resemble a paper airplane. Let's take a look:

### The Major Pentatonic "Airplane":

The illustration below shows the pattern created by the first four notes of the Major Pentatonic scale. As you can see, the pattern resembles a paper airplane flying 'right-side-up'.

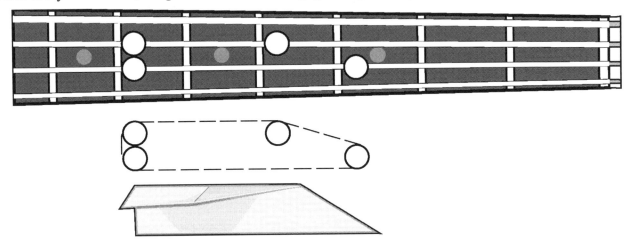

### The Minor Pentatonic Airplane:

The illustration below shows the pattern created by the first four notes of the Minor Pentatonic scale. As you can see, the pattern resembles a paper airplane flying 'upside-down'.

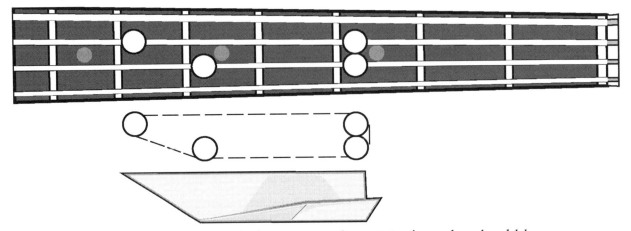

The reasoning behind using paper airplanes to teach pentatonic scales should become apparent in the examples that follow.

Before we dig in to the Pentatonic Scale pattern on 2 strings, let's review the paper airplane as a visual pattern substitute:

*Major Pentatonic "Airplane":*

*Minor Pentatonic "Airplane":*

So, without further fanfare or delay, here is the Pentatonic Scale pattern on 2 strings:

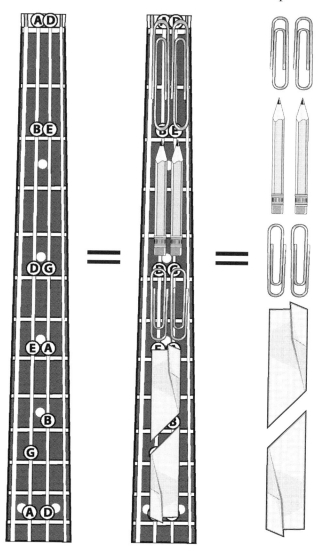

The scale shown on the bass fingerboard above can be either an E Minor Pentatonic scale or a G Major Pentatonic scale. Either way, the pattern above works for both. Using the paper clip, pencil, and paper airplane icons will reveal another pattern when we take a look at how the above pattern repeats.

Chapter 13 - The Pentatonic Scale - Analyzing the Pentatonic Super Scale

# The 2 String Pentatonic Pattern (repeating)

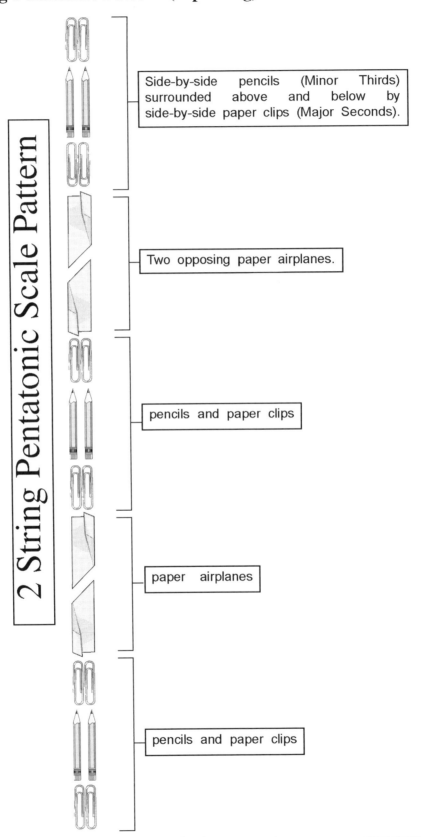

- Side-by-side pencils (Minor Thirds) surrounded above and below by side-by-side paper clips (Major Seconds).
- Two opposing paper airplanes.
- pencils and paper clips
- paper airplanes
- pencils and paper clips

You should also be aware of the five sub-patterns that exist in the 4-string Master Pentatonic Pattern. Being aware of these sub-patterns will help you to more easily memorize the overall pattern.

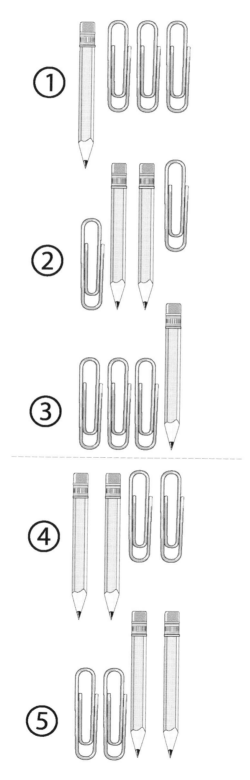

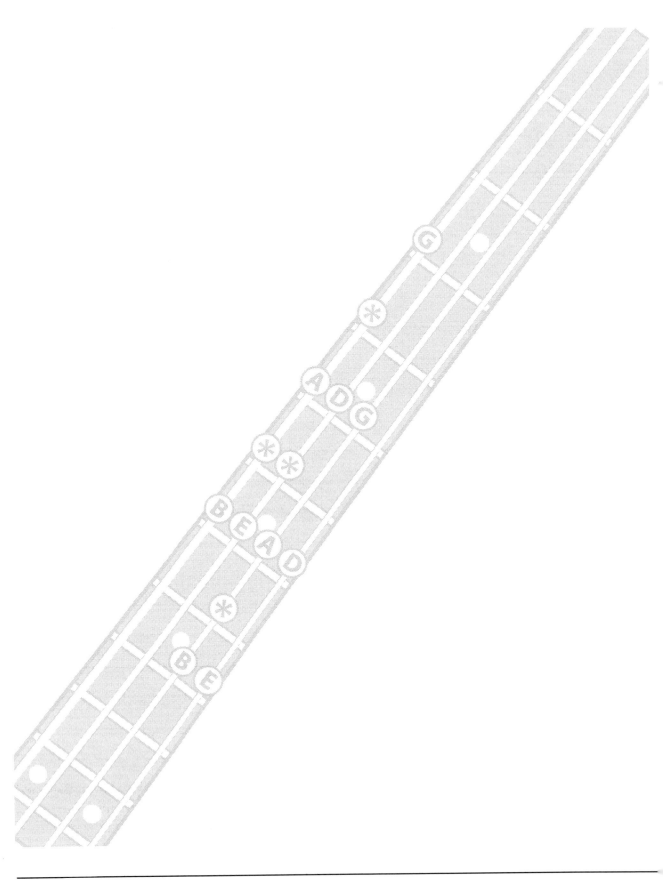

# Chapter 14: Non-Diatonic Notes & Scales

Jazz, blues, and rock musicians often employ "blues notes" and "passing tones" that fall outside the diatonic notes contained in the modes, or the notes contained in the pentatonic scale. Some of these non-diatonic notes are just notes that fall between scale tones, while others are organized into non-diatonic scales. In this section, we'll explore the use of blues notes and passing tones on the bass. We'll also take a look at a few of the non-diatonic scales: the Whole Tone scale, the Chromatic scale, and the Harmonic and Melodic Minor scales.

## Blues Notes

As you may have guessed, Blues Notes derive their name from the blues players who raised their use to an art form. Blues notes provide the bassist with a way to breathe new life into common scales. Blues notes provide a loose feel that can almost make it sound as if you're bending your bass strings while playing, when in fact, you're not bending them at all. (Okay... maybe a little.)

In the illustration below, which shows an E Minor Pentatonic scale in root position, the note dot with the asterisk ($*$) is a blues note - in this case a "Flat 5th". The Flat 5th is one of the most commonly used blues notes. (A Pentatonic Scale with a Flat 5th is also referred to as a "Blues Scale".)

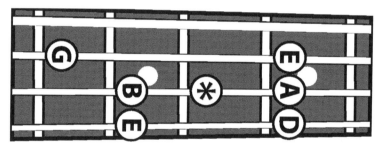

Another, less commonly used blues note is the "Flat 9" (or Flat 2). The example below shows both the Flat 2 and Flat 9 represented by the note dots with the asterisks ($*$) as applied to the E Minor Pentatonic Scale.

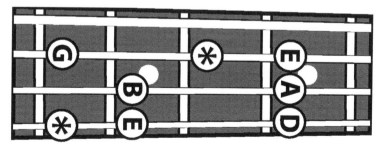

## Passing Tones /Passing Notes

Passing Tones (or passing notes) are notes in between the Diatonic notes which, when included in your bass lines, add melodic interest and color. Classical composers and jazz musicians alike have long employed passing tones with skill to create more beautiful and interesting melodies.

Almost any note that falls between the Diatonic/Pentatonic scale tones can be used as a Passing Note. In the illustration below, the note dots with the asterisk (∗) represent a series of passing notes.

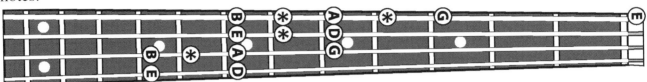

While this example shows a series of passing tones used in conjunction with the E Minor Pentatonic Scale, any note between any scale tone can be used as a passing tone. Passing notes are used extensively by Jazz bassists who play "walking" basslines. Passing tones also work well as "leading tones", which are passing notes a half step above or below a diatonic note (usually the root) used to create harmonic tension that will lead the listener to anticipate a resolution note.

## The Whole Tone Scale

The Whole Tone scale is a scale that is constructed using only whole steps, which is undoubtedly why it's called the "whole tone" scale. Because of its unique construction, this scale has 6 notes. Take a look at the illustration of the whole tone scale below:

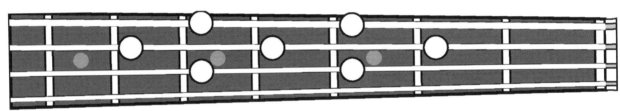

The whole tone scale is a good match when you need a bassline to accompany an augmented chord. Also, don't overlook the whole tone scale as a way to break out of diatonic playing from time to time while adding interest to your playing.

## The Chromatic Scale

The Chromatic Scale is basically all 12 notes from root to octave. While some might argue that a chromatic scale is no scale at all because it has no structure, chromatic playing can add a whole new dimension to your sound if used in moderation; too much chromatic playing and your band members might want to kick you out. Take a look at the illustration of the chromatic scale below:

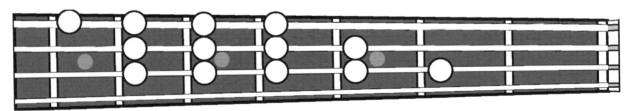

Any scale takes a lot of practice to use with authority, but because there is no structure to the chromatic scale, chromatic playing can be more difficult to master. As with the whole tone scale, chromatic playing can enable you to break free from playing only diatonic notes.

# The Harmonic Minor Scale

The Harmonic Minor Scale is basically a Natural Minor Scale (an Aeolian Mode) with a "Sharp 7th", or raised seventh scale tone. This raised 7th allows the Harmonic Minor scale to have some of the properties of a Minor scale, and some of the properties of a Major scale, namely, the "leading tone" seventh note, which is a half step below the root note (as in the Major scale).

Below is an example of the Harmonic Minor Scale:

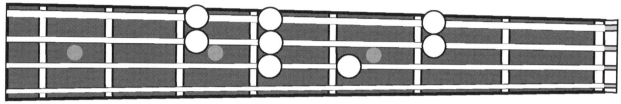

The raised 7th is referred to as a "leading tone", because it "leads" the listeners ear back to the root, or tonic, or key center note.

# The Melodic Minor Scale

The Melodic Minor Scale is one scale on the way up, and another on the way down. On the way up, the "ascending" Melodic Minor Scale is like a Dorian mode with a "Sharp 7th", or raised seventh scale tone.

Below is an example of the ascending Melodic Minor Scale:

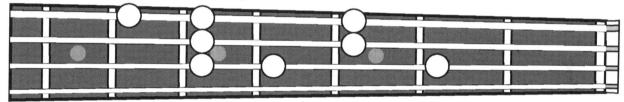

However, on the way down (descending), the Melodic Minor Scale reverts back to the humble Natural Minor Scale, as shown below:

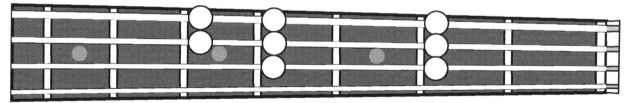

Both the Harmonic and Melodic Minor scales have been used by classical composers for their unique properties, so even though they might seem a bit strange at first, you can bet that a lot of thought went into the notes that comprise these two hybrid scales.

Chapter 14 - Non-Diatonic Scales

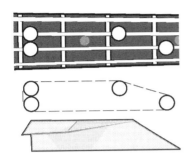  
 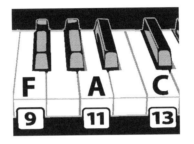 
 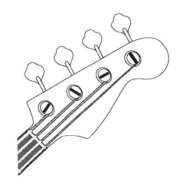 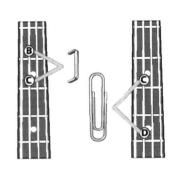
 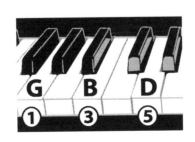 

# Conclusion

While there are many schools of thought when it comes to the subject of music, the real judge of any music is the listener. No matter how technically perfect or imperfect the music is, or how well or poorly it stands up to the analysis of Music Theory, and regardless of the proficiency level of the musicians who create that music, the bottom line when it comes to Music is this:

## If it sounds good, it is good!!

With music, you have infinite choices. The purpose of this book is to narrow the infinite choices down to a starting point. The lessons here are not meant to limit you to playing only diatonic notes. You can use the blues notes, passing notes, and chromatic notes anytime you want to. The purpose of this information is to give you a foundation. Knowledge of diatonic harmony and music theory (chords, modes, key signatures,...) is a great tool to use when creating your own music or communicating with other musicians.

## Improvisation

Improvising, or making up what you play as you play it, is a technique that's used by rock, jazz, and blues musicians throughout the world. Understanding how to match modes or pentatonic scales with chords is at the heart of musical improvisation. Once you understand the diatonic harmony structure, you can see the correlation between chord types and mode types. However, there's no need to limit your note choices strictly to scale tones, modal tones, and chord tones. There are many notes in between the diatonic tones that lend color interest to your playing. Examples of these "outside" notes are the "blues" notes – a flat 2 (or flat 9), or a flat 5 – or the use of passing tones – the notes in between the scale tones played chromatically to add interest. Additionally, there are numerous non-diatonic scales that are commonly used to add interest to music, such as the Whole Tone Scale – a 6 note scale that uses only whole steps, and no half steps.

After reading this book, continue studying music as a way to improve your bass playing. Practice the scale and arpeggio patterns presented throughout the book. Learn about Melodic Devices such as answer/echo, expansion, diminution, sequencing, and melodic reflection as a way to create more interesting and melodic basslines. Keep on learning!

Sticking to Modes and Diatonic Harmony is not the pinnacle of understanding music – it's just a solid starting point. So once you learn the basics, never be afraid to move "outside" of the dictates of Diatonic Harmony.

Thank you for purchasing this book.

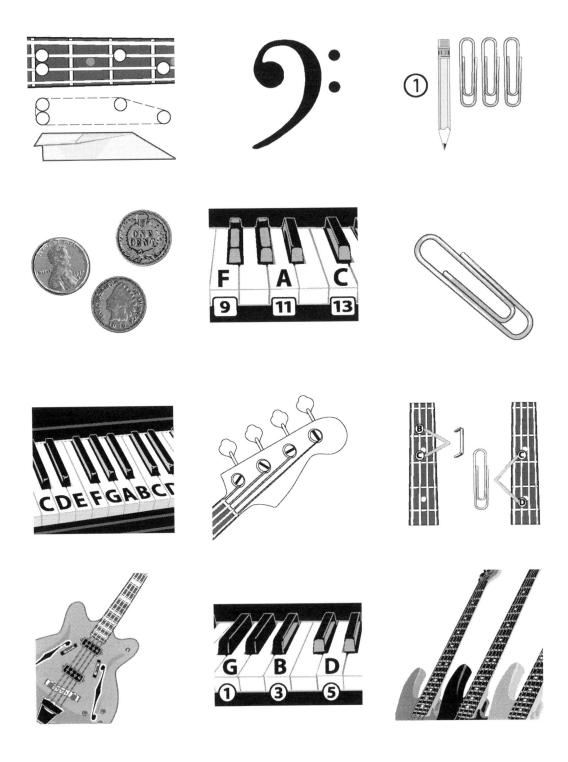

Made in the USA
Middletown, DE
04 January 2019